I Remember Lemuria
and
The Return of Sathanas

Princess Vanue, from the original Amazing Stories printing of
"I Remember Lemuria!"

Richard S. Shaver

I Remember Lemuria
and
The Return of Sathanas

BIBLIOBAZAAR

Copyright © 2008 BiblioBazaar
All rights reserved

Original copyright: 1948

I Remember Lemuria
AND
The Return of Sathanas

CONTENTS

FOREWORD..9

I REMEMBER LEMURIA

I.	City of the Titans	15
II.	From Art to Embryology	25
III.	Terror in Tean City	35
IV.	Escape Into Space	45
V.	The Princess Vanue	57
VI.	Conclave of the Elders	66
VII.	A Wedding on Nor	72
VIII.	Return to Mu	81
IX.	The Abandondero	88
X.	Into the Tunnels of the Dero	96
XI.	Battle to the Death	104

THE RETURN OF SATHANAS

I.	Quest of the Darkome	117
II.	Whence Came Sathanas?	122
III.	Back on Mother Mu	128
IV.	Pact with the Aesir	137
V.	War Against the Jotuns	149
VI.	In the Hands of Sathanas	161
VII.	A Valuable Chunk of Meat	166

VIII.	Under The Pain Ray	172
IX.	Seizing the Satana	179
X.	A Satanic Hostage	189
XI.	Plot Against Pandral	199
XII.	Harald's Hostages	211

Mr. Shaver's Lemurian Alphabet 215

FOREWORD

Perhaps my parents never realized the puns that would be made on my name when they christened me Richard Sharpe Shaver. Under ordinary circumstances the puns would have been of little consequence, but because of the amazing fact of my amazing memory of the life of another person, long dead, it has been incredibly hard for me to speak convincingly and to make people believe in me. Invariably I get that oh-so-funny remark, "Sharp-shaver, eh? A regular cut-up, eh, kid!" accompanied by a sly dig in the ribs and a very stupid, "Get it?" How can a man get a serious audience after that?

And yet, there it is for all who wish—to pun and pun again. If I achieve nothing else at least you may laugh, and to laugh is to be physically and mentally healthy. For those of you who will read on and carefully weigh what I am about to tell you I am convinced there will be no thought of puns. Instead, when you consider the real truths behind what I say—and even better, experiment and study to corroborate them—it seems to me to be inevitable that you will forget that I am Richard Sharpe Shaver, and instead, am what science chooses to very vaguely define as the racial memory receptacle of a man (or should I say a being?) named Mutan Mion, who lived many thousands of years ago in Sub Atlan, one of the great cities of ancient Lemuria!

I myself cannot explain it. I know only that I remember Lemuria! Remember it with a faithfulness that I accept with the absolute conviction of a fanatic. And yet, I am not a fanatic; I am a simple man, a worker in metal, employed in a steel mill in Pennsylvania. I am as normal as any of you who read this and gifted with much less imagination than most of you!

What I tell you is not fiction! How can I impress that on you as forcibly as I feel it must be impressed? But then. what good to impress it upon those who will crack wise about me being a "sharp-shaver"? I can only hope that when I have told the story of Mutan Mion as I remember it you will believe—not because I sound convincing or tell my story in a convincing manner, but because you will see the truth in what I say, and will realize, as you must, that many of the things I tell you are not a matter of present day scientific knowledge and yet are true!

I fervently hope that such great minds as Einstein, Carrel, and the late Crile check the things that I remember. I am no mathematician; I am no scientist. I have studied all the scientific books I can get—only to become more and more convinced that I remember true things. But surely someone can definitely say that I am wrong or that I am right, especially in such things as the true nature of gravity, or matter, of light, of the cause of age and many other things that the memory of Mutan Mion has expressed to me so definitely as to be conviction itself.

I intend to put down these things, and I invite—challenge!—any of you to work on them; to prove or disprove, as you like. Whatever your goal, I do not care. I care only that you believe me or disbelieve me with enough fervor to do some real work on those things I will propound. The final result may well stagger the science of the world.

I want to thank editor Ray Palmer, in whose "fiction" magazine, Amazing Stories, the stories in this book were first published, for his open mind and for the way he has received the things I have told him in addition to what I have written in this story of Mutan Mion of ancient Lemuria. It began when he published my ancient alphabet in "Discussions"[1] and requested the readers to carry out checks of their own. I myself did not realize the extent of the alphabetic (more properly phonetic) language. But surely there must be tremendous significance in the fact that the alphabet fits into every language to which it has been applied, to the amazing percentage of 75% in the German to 94% in the ancient Egyptian! Even in Chinese and Japanese it ranked consistent nine out of ten times.

To me it is tragic that the only way I can tell my story is in the guise of fiction. And yet, I am thankful for the opportunity to do even this; and to editor Ray Palmer I express my unbounded gratitude. I know that if even a few of you go to the lengths he has gone to check many of the things I remember, a beginning will have been made to something, the ending of which (if ending there is) awes me beyond my poor power to express my feelings.

—RICHARD S. SHAVER.

Footnotes

1   January, 1945 issue of AMAZING STORIES. Some of the reports by readers were subsequently published, but the great majority were not. These reports proved to be the most amazing the editor has ever received on anything published in his magazine. They would seem to indicate beyond all doubt that the "ancient language" of Mr. Shaver is part of an original "mother tongue" from which all Earthly language, have sprung. For example, the name Mutan Mion, broken down into the letters and sounds of this ancient language becomes MU—"man"; T—"integration," "growth"; AN—"animal." MION means "manchild seed." So the name means "man spore cultured to new forms by integration growth forces." In other words, a synthetic mutation by the use of force or rays.—Ed.

I REMEMBER LEMURIA

Thought Records from the
Past Tell the Ancient
Story of Lemuria which
Some Call Mu or Pan

—By Richard S. Shaver

CHAPTER I.

CITY OF THE TITANS

I was working in the studio of Artan Gro when I heard a great laugh behind me. If ever there was derision in a laugh, there was derision in this one. I flung down my gaudy brushes and my palette and turned about in a rage—to find the master himself, his red cave of a mouth wide open in his black beard. I cooled my temper with an effort; for great indeed is Artan Gro, master artist of Sub Atlan.

"I am sorry, Mutan Mion," he gasped, "but I can't control my laughter. No one ever has conceived, much less executed, anything worse than what you have put upon canvas! What do you call it, 'Proteus in a Convulsive Nightmare'?"

But Artan Gro could control himself, I was sure. It is one of the things I have learned of the really great in the arts; they make no pretenses. He was laughing because he wanted to tell me frankly what he thought of my ability as an artist. It is bad enough when your friends mock your work (and they had), but when the master is convulsed with laughter it is high time to wake up to the truth.

"It is true, great Artan Gro," I said humbly. "I want to paint but I cannot. I haven't the ability."

Artan Gro's expression softened. He smiled, and as he smiled it was as though he had turned on the sunlight.

"Go," he said, "go; to the deeper caverns at Mu's center. Once there study science; learn to mix the potions that give the brain greater awareness, a better rate of growth." He patted my shoulder and added a last bit of advice. "Once you have mixed the potions, take them. Drink them—and grow!" He passed on, still chuckling.

Why is the truth always so brutal? Or does it just seem brutal when it comes from those wiser than you? I slunk from the studio; but I had already determined to take his advice. I would go to Tean City, at Mu's center. I would go to the science schools of the Titans.

Never before had I considered leaving Sub Atlan, my birthplace, or as I should express it, my growth place, for I am a culture man, a product of the laboratories. In fact, I remember no other place on Mu, although it is a fact that during the process of my development to culture manhood,

I roamed the culture forests of Atlantis, [2] which is the name for Surface Atlan. Sub Atlan is just below Atlantis, while Tean City is located at the center of Mu, at a great depth below Sub Atlan. The walls of the great cavern in which Tean City is located are hardened to untellable strength by treatment with ray-flows which feed its growth until it is of great density. There are many other cities which grew through the centuries to vast size, but none so great as Tean City. Some are abandoned, but all are indestructible; their cavern walls too dense to penetrate or to collapse.

Since Tean City is located near the center of Mother Mu, gravity neutralizes itself by opposition. It is very comfortable. Many of the Titans live there, and in fact, it is almost a Titan city. There also are the mighty ones, the Elders of the Atlan race's government. Huge they are, like great trees, many centuries old and still growing. I had long wished to see them, and now that I had decided to go, the thrill was greater than any I had ever experienced, I was going down into the city of many wonders!

Out on the street I took one of the many vehicles that are provided for travel about the city. These vehicles, their weight reduced by a gravity deflection device, are powered by motors whose energy is derived from a gravity focusing magnetic field, by which one side of a flywheel becomes much heavier than the other. This is accomplished by bending gravity fall [3] in the same way that a lens bends a light ray.

The topless [4] buildings of Sub Atlan fled by me; and soon I neared the squat entrance to the shafts that fell from Sub Atlan to Center Mu, to Tean City, home of the Titans. [5] I knew that swift elevators dropped down these shafts; but I had never traveled in one of them.

Because I knew the control-man of one of the elevators, having talked with him often of Tean City and the wonders he had seen in it, I went to his shaft for my descent. He was glad to see me, and very much surprised to learn that I was going to Tean City.

"You will never regret it!" he declared.

The car dropped sickeningly, so swiftly that a great fear grew in me that I would be crushed by deceleration when we finally stopped. In panic I watched an indicator's two hands move slowly toward each other as though to cover its face in shame. Then, with little sensation, the car stopped. Here at the center of Mu I had become nearly weightless and the ceasing of even such swift motion did not have ill effects upon my weightless body. I knew that I would not have that fear again.

Two fat Atlans stepped out of the car ahead of me, sighing with relief at their renewed weightlessness, which they had obviously been anticipating. As I was about to follow them from the car, the control-man drew me aside.

"Fear rides the ways down here," he whispered, his sharp-pointed, cat-like ears quivering an alert. "Fear is a smell down here that is ever in the nose—a bad smell, too. Try to figure it out while you are down here; and tell me, too, if you get an answer."

I did not understand what he meant, but I promised anyway. The smell of fear, in Tean City?

Immediately I was immersed in the sensually shocking appeal of a variform crowd, mostly at this hour, a shopping rush of female variforms. While there were many of my own type, and of the elevator control-man's type, there were a greater number of creatures of every shape the mind could grasp and some that it could not. All were citizens; all were animate and intelligent—hybrids of every race that space crossing had ever brought into contact, from planets whose very names are now lost in time. The technicons may have been wrong in the opinion of some when they developed variform breeding; but they have certainly given life variety. I had never seen so many variforms [6] before.

At a corner of the vastly vaulted way where many rollat platforms [7] crossed and recrossed each other, I stepped to a telescreen and dialed the student center. The image of a tremendous six-armed Sybyl female filled the screen and the electrically augmented body appeal of the mighty life within her seized the youth in me and wrung it as no embrace from lesser female ever had.

"And what" her voice shook me as a leaf in an organ pipe "might a pale and puny male like you want in Tean City? You look as if you never had enough to eat, as if love had passed you by. Did you come down here because no one wanted you elsewhere?"

I grinned self-consciously back at her image, my voice a feeble piping in comparison to hers.

"I have come to learn something beside drawing lines around dreams. I am a painter from the subsurface who has decided that knowledge of actual growth is more important than the false growth of an untrue image upon a canvas." I wondered what the master would have said to hear me.

"You are right," she boomed back, her six arms engaged in complex wand mysterious movements, picking up and laying down instruments and tools in bewildering rapidity, her attention elsewhere yet enough remaining on me to hold me bound in an attraction as strong as a towing cable. She was a forty foot Titan, her age unknown. As I thought upon this and tried not to think of the immense beauty and life force of her, I suddenly realized she was hiding fear. I have a peculiar faculty for sensing hidden emotions. That bluff greeting had been a hidden wish to drive me from some danger. But I did not speak of it, for I read that caution in her; a very strong mental flow that fairly screamed DON'T.

This kind of fear was a wonder and a new thing to me, for danger was a thing long banished from our life. Then she spoke, reluctantly it seemed.

"Go to the center of the Hall of Symbols. There you can ask a student or an instructor who will tell you all you need to know."

The grip of the woman life in her left my mind and she was gone from my vision. As I turned from the telescreen my mind insisted on visualizing that six-armed embrace and its probable effect upon a man in love. I shivered in spite of the warmth, but not from fear. The blood of the Titans was alive, I thought; strangely and wonderfully alive!

I stepped into a rollat at the curb, inspected the directory, then inserted a coin and dialed the number of the building that housed the Hall of Symbols. I leaned back while the automatic drive of the rollat directed the car through the speeding traffic, its electric eye more efficient than my own.

Yes, much more efficient than my own at the moment, which were wandering over the figure of a variform female on the walk whose upper part was the perfect torso of a woman and whose lower part was a sinuously gliding thirty feet of brilliantly mottled snake. You could never have escaped her embrace of your own will once she had wrapped those life-generating coils around you!

I thought upon it. The gen of these variforms was certainly more vital; possibly because the Titan technicons Who lived here kept the people healthier. Perhaps the hybrids were naturally more fecund of microspore. It had indeed been a day of brainstorms, I mused, when some old technicon had realized that not only would a strong integrative field with a rich exd ^{8} supply cause all matter to grow at an increased rate, but would also cause even the most dissimilar life-gens to unite. It has been the realization that had resulted in various form life. Most of the crosses by this method had resulted in an increased strength and fertility. They now were more numerous than four-limbed men, and often superior in mental ability.

Automatically my mind associated the embrace of the snake woman with the six arms of the giant Sybyl of Info; and I decided that I understood why Artan Gro had driven me here with his scorn. If I didn't learn about life here I never would anywhere. That had been what he had reasoned.

Soon I was striding between the pillaring fangs of the great beast's mouth that was the door of the Hall of Symbols where the school ways converged. About was the bustle attendant to any rollat way station; bearers rushing; travelers gazing about lost in wonder at the vaulting glitter of sculptured pillars and painted walls, done by men of a calibre whose work ro [9] like myself cannot grasp entirely.

Paintings and sculpture here hammered into the brain a message of the richness of life that immense mutual effort can give the lift unit, the pro. This richness of life was pictured in a terrible clash with evil, its opposite. [10] The hot fecundity of life and health growth was a sensuous blow upon the eyes, the soul leaped to take a hand and make life yet more worthwhile. I could not cease gazing at the leaping vault of pictured busy figures whose movements culminated in that offer to the spirit of man to join them in moulding life to a fit shape.

My rapt study of the paintings was interrupted by the sound of a pair of hooves that clicked daintily to a stop beside me. I glanced at the newcomer, who had stopped to stare up at the paintings also in that curious way that people have when they see another craning his neck— and my glance became a stare.

What was the use of aspiring to be an artist, my reason said, if those great masters who had placed that mighty picture book on the vaulting walls above were so easily outdone by the life force itself!

She was but a girl, younger than myself, but what a girl! Her body was encased in a transparent glitter; her skin a rosy pale purple; her legs, mottled with white, ended in a pair of cloven hooves. And as my brain struggled to grasp her colorful young perfection—she wagged her tail!

It was all too much. Speculating about the life-generating force possible in the variform creatures was one thing; but having it materialize beside you was another thing entirely. Such a beautiful tail it was. Of the softest, most beautiful fur.

"What were you staring at?" she asked. "The paintings?"

I stuttered, then answered. "The paintings . . . I guess . . . yes, the paintings. I'm a . . . painter . . . was a painter . . ." I gave up. I couldn't talk, I had to look.

"They are marvelous, aren't they," she declared enthusiastically. "I always look at them when I come down to the school. I am studying medicine. Now take that painting up there—"

On her arm and breast I saw the medical school insignia; a man's figure struggling with a great snake, disease.[11] It took brains to study medicine. This exquisite young thing, so full of gen force, so powerfully attractive, was smart too. And almost instantly she proved herself to be extremely friendly and companionable. She went on talking, describing, theorizing in a gush of amiable conversation that left me dizzy, gasping, and admiringly breathless. She told me everything about the paintings, the statues.

And before I realized it, we were walking on together. She was full of all sorts of information, and it seemed she had taken it upon herself to be my guide, to teach me the meaning of everything we saw. Her cheerful chatter soon told me all about herself, her studies, the schools, the great doors that led to each one from the central gathering place of the school rollat ways.

The Hall was justly famous for these doors. Before us now was the door to the medical school, formed of pillaring figures struggling with the coils of snakes. Next to it was the marine school door, formed of a crab whose huge claws met to form the arch. A planetron, a pendulum device to tell of the nearness of bodies in space, formed the entrance to the school of space navigation. All the ages of science of immortal growth had combined here in the symbols that formed the many doors.

Footnotes

2   According to Plato, Atlantis was a continent located some four hundred miles west of the Pillars of Hercules (Gibraltar). In the Timaeus, he describes it as an island larger than Asia Minor combined with Libya. Beyond it, he says, were an archipelago of lesser islands. Atlantis had been a powerful kingdom nine thousand years before the birth of Solon (from whom Plato heard of Atlantis reputedly as told to Solon by Egyptian priests), and its armies had overrun the Mediterranean lands, when Athens alone had resisted. (It has been a point of difference between students as to whether Plato referred to the "Mediterranean lands" as lands now inundated by the Mediterranean Sea, or the lands surrounding the sea.) Finally the sea overwhelmed Atlantis and shoals marked the spot. In the Critias Plato gives a history of the commonwealth of Atlantis.

There are many other traditions of lands located west of Gibraltar. The Greek Isles of the Blest or Fortunate Isles; the Welsh Avalon; the Portuguese Antilia or Isle of Seven Cities; and St. Brendan's island. All except Avalon were marked on maps of the 14th and 15th centuries.

The legends of the Sargasso Sea are said to have sprung from encounters with the sea of weeds which periodically grew over the shallowly sunken continent.—Ed.

3   The reader will note the curious use of the word "fall" in connection with gravity. Later in the story, the author elaborates on the subject of gravity in a very amazing manner, propounding a theory which your editor has examined in detail and by which he has been utterly confounded. This glib "focusing" and "deflecting" of gravity your editor cautions you to accept in the literal sense until Mu-tan Mion's story gives us more on the subject of gravity.—Ed.

4   Curious as to the literal meaning of the word "topless" we wrote to Mr. Shaver for a better description of the buildings of Sub Atlan. He revealed that (as Mutan Mion's memory told him) they were topless in the sense that they were roofless. Sub Atlan is located in one of the giant near-surface caverns that underlie Surface Atlan, or Atlantis, which is mostly forest with scattered large buildings. Since the elements are not a factor, almost all buildings are constructed without roofs to admit a maximum of light. Sub Atlan must have presented a strange appearance, for no two buildings were architecturally alike; some of them huge spheres, or multi-sided geometric shapes, tall spires,

or merely rambling structures of no apparent intentional design. The reason for this was to provide variety to interest the eye, which would otherwise be jaded by constant contemplation of the unending sameness of gray cavern walls and roof of stone.—Ed.

5 When asked to describe the Titans Mr. Shaver sent us the following notation, which is perhaps the oddest of all his communications. When queried about its oddity, he merely replied that he had "answered your question" and gave no further explanation. We quote:

"Our great race, the Atlans, together with the Titans, our allies and often our fellow citizens, swarm through all known space and watch ever for the birth of new suns. Then, too, there are the Nortans; but the Nor-men shun all suns and can only be found where the sun rays shine not.

"When our Atlan sciencons hear of or see a new sun born, our ships flash swiftly through the void, to test the rays for poisonous emanations. When they find clean heat from a surface shell of pure carbon, fast upon their trail come the first great colonization ships. For our race is fecund beyond imagination and there is little death from any cause."

Obviously this is nothing from the "racial" memory of Mutan Mion, but seemingly something from an Atlan himself! Here and there, through Mr. Shaver's correspondence with the editors, such departures from the identity of Mutan Mion occur, and we can only suggest that Mr. Shaver's racial memory contacts extend not only to the culture man, but to other beings as well. Mr. Shaver himself cannot explain, and in many instances, is unaware, that such extensions exist.

The reader will here, again, note several inexplicable references. such as "poisonous emanations" and "a surface shell of pure carbon." Later in the story Mutan Mion tells of these things in great detail, and in them gives still another of the amazing scientific theories that stagger the imagination.—Ed.

6 Obviously variforms are not natives of other planets, but hybrids developed from many interplanetary life forms mated with Titans and Atlans by deliberate applications of mutative rays in the laboratories of Mu's technicons. It is extremely interesting to note that all have the status of citizens.—Ed.

7 Moving connected vehicles on the ways and walks which carried the bulk of pedestrian travel.—Ed.

8   Exd is Atlan for ex-disintegrance or energy ash. It was the principal content of the beneficial vibrants. It is the space dust from which all matter grows into being. Mutan Mion amplifies the exd theory later on in the story.—Ed.

9   Here again we had to appeal to Mr. Shaver for amplification. We certainly got it, and along with it some amazing thoughts. Ro (he says) is a thing of simple repetitive life pattern easy to understand and control. To ro you is to make you do things against your will. A large generator of thought impulse can be set up to ro a whole group of people. Row the boat is modern and the meaning has become physical force and not mental force. Ro the people was an ancient method of government. Romantic was the name of such a government. Ro-man-tic (science of man life patterning by control). It is the same concept as used by some scientists when they say "hypnotically conditioned." It is not necessarily an evil government method, but is one that was necessary. Any person is ro who is weaker than the mental impulses about him. Men are ro today because they are not self-determining, though they think they are. We are parts of a huge juggernaut, and we are ro in consequence. The determining forces that make our thought what it is are from outside when we are ro, from inside when we are men or gods.—Ed.

10 This is indeed a strange comparison. Evil is the opposite of live, the inference being that to be evil is to die. Oddly (or significantly?) evil is live spelled backward.—Ed.

11 This insignia lives today in the legend of Apollo! According to the Greeks, Apollo was a son of Zeus himself. Disease is typified in the legend by the python, which Apollo killed. Etymologically his name signifies one who "drives away disease." Roscher's derivation names him as the "sun god." Using Mr. Shaver's ancient language, he is "authority, energizer, power source of man's growth." This is startling when we discover, upon studying the legends of Apollo, that he was variously called god of prophecy; god of agriculture; ruler of seasons; keeper of flocks; rearer of boys; sponsor of gymnastics; the helper; healer and seer; averter of evil; god of song and music; leader of the muses; embarker and disembarker; god of streets and ways; one who stands before the house (as protector from violence and disease); originator and protector of civil order; founder of cities and legislation. Apollo, says Mutan Mion, was a son of one of the Titans of Mu!—Ed.

CHAPTER II.

FROM ART TO EMBRYOLOGY

From the moment that I pocketed a disc that bore the faun-legged girl's name and address, I was no longer an aspiring artist; I wanted to know what she knew, wanted to learn what she was learning.

Arl was her name, a short, sweet name for a girl and hard to forget, too. You can't forget a girl who wags her tail at you just like that.

And so she took me into the medical school and directed me to her own teacher. I became a member of the class immediately and discovered that I had entered upon the opening discourse.

The class was dominated by the immense presence of the teacher, a son of the Titans, bearded and horned, expounding in the exact syllogism of the technicon training. As he spoke, I became certain that this dynamo of human force should soon charge such a small battery as myself with everything in the way of knowledge I could assimilate.

There was only one slight disturbing factor. Just as I had sensed a strange, deeply buried and secret fear in the Sybyl, I knew that in the mind of this great son of the Titans there was a gnawing something that a part of his brain dwelt on continually. Fear was a smell that was ever in the nose down here in Tean City. The realization disturbed me so much that I failed to absorb a portion of the teacher's discourse. My absorption must have caught his attention, too, for I saw him staring disapprovingly at me. With a start, I re-concentrated my mind on what he was saying.

" . . . a great cold ball hung in space. Once it had been a mighty, living planet, swinging ponderously around a dying sun that it had never seen, being covered with clouds. Then that sun had gone out, and the deadly ter [12] stiffened the surface life into glittering death.

"The planet's forests, which had lived in dense, dripping fog, had, in their many ages of life, deposited coal beds untold miles in depth—clear down to the stony core of the planet. No fire had ever touched these forests, because the dense fog had never allowed fire to burn.

"Venus, our nearest neighbor in space, is such a planet now, although much smaller. As it is on Venus, so it was on the unknown planet.

"Hanging in space the dead immensity of this ball was largely potential heat, for its tremendously thick shell was mostly pure carbon.

"Such once was the sun, your sun and mine; the sun of which Mu is a daughter.

"Then a blazing meteor, spewed violently from some sun in space, came flaming toward this cold ball. Deep it plunged into the beds of carbon. The fire spread swiftly—an ever-fire of disintegrance, not the passing-fire of combustion—and our sun was born into live-giving flame!

"A carbon fire is a clean fire and contains no dense metals like radium, titanium, uranium, polonium—whose emanations in disintegrance in suns cause old age and death because minute particles given off accumulate and convey the ever-fire into the body, there to kill it in time.

"Then sun heat was clean, and life sprang furiously into being on its daughter, Mu's surface. Nor did this life die—death came only by being eaten. Then life suffered old age not at all, for there was no cause."

The voice of the teacher paused a moment, and now indeed I knew that there was much for me to learn. Here was something that struck deep into me with an instantly vital interest. Most provoking of all was his peculiar emphasis on the word "then." I could not help the question that sprang to my lips.

"Why do you say 'Then life suffered old age not at all, for there was no cause.'? Is there cause now?"

It was as though I had placed a torch beneath the hidden fear in the Titan's eyes, for it flamed forth suddenly for all to see; but it was as quickly quelled. All in the class looked at me with that shocked expression which plainly said I had overstepped my bounds; but in the eyes of Arl I thought I saw the gleam of approval, and I found a dam to hold back my ebbing courage.

The teacher looked at me, and I saw kindliness in his eyes.

"You are new here, Mutan Mion. Therefore it is easy to understand that you have not heard of the projected migration of all Atlans to a new world under a beneficial sun . . .

"Yes, young ro, there is cause." He was answering my question with determination now, but he was not speaking to me alone; he was making his answer a part of his discourse. "I have spoken of the carbon fire as a clean fire. By this I mean that the atoms of carbon, when disintegrated, send forth the beneficial energy ash called exd which can be assimilated by our bodies and used to promote life-growth. However, the source of this ash is not carbon alone, but all other elements excepting the heavy metals such as I mentioned before. It is when these heavy elements begin to disintegrate in the ever-fire that we come to the cause of age.

"The particles of radium and other radioactive metals are the poison that causes the aging of tissue. These particles are thrown out by all old suns whose shell of carbon has been partly or altogether burned away, permitting the disintegrating fire to reach and seize upon the heavy metals at the sun's core. Our sun has begun to throw out great masses of these poisonous particles. They fall upon Mu in a continual flood, entering into living tissue and infecting it with the radioactive disease we call age.

"Through the years, the centuries, these poisons accumulate in the soil of the planet, and are continually being washed out of it by the rains with the result that all the water on Mu is becoming increasingly contaminated. When these waters are drunk, the poisons accumulate in the body, finally becoming numerous enough to completely halt all growth and still worse, to prevent any effectual use of exd, which is the food of all integration.

"The technicons, of course, have devised means to protect us from the accumulation of the age poisons, but it has become evident that their efforts are not entirely foolproof. We have discovered that we are living on a world that circles a sun that is growing old and is therefore deadly. We are living in the shadow of death, a shadow that will grow greater as the years pass until finally death with strike us all. We would, if we remained, not even begin to live out our lives. Centuries and centuries would be lost to us, and ultimately we might not even attain the initial growth of maturity!"

I ventured another question.

"What methods have the technicons devised?"

"They are simple ones. Multiple distillation of the water in which we drink and bathe; treatment of the water in a centrifuge to remove the very finely divided age poisons that cannot be removed by distillation; ben generators to create a magnetic field of ben energies; air centrifuges to remove poisons from the air. But I must impress upon you that it is impossible to shield us from all of the age poison; from that small amount that actually falls upon our own bodies and accumulates there as it does in the water. Eventually, if we remain on Mu, we will grow old, [13] and finally die."

I looked him squarely in the eyes, respectful in a degree equal to the kindly interest that shone in his as he returned my look.

"It is not the age poisons you fear," I accused.

He looked at me silently; and a flood of force seemed to flow through me, encouraging me, protecting me, cautioning me. It was the same feeling I had gotten from the Sybyl.

"Come, students," he said gently. "We will go now to the embryo laboratory."

Before we entered the laboratory we were given nutrient potions prescribed by the Titan for his students to make them more receptive and hence his work easier. We were told that we would receive these potions regularly. Even as I took the first draught my brain throbbed with a new growth of ideas and strange new images. I was exhilarated beyond all imagining, and my enthusiasm knew no bounds. I took Arl's hand in mine as we trooped into the laboratory.

It was truly a wonderful place, the most amazing I had ever seen. I felt like a mite admitted to the treasure-house of a giant. Here were things that were beyond my intelligence to create of my own mind power; and yet I was being given free and welcome access to all of them, to learn from them, and to use the knowledge if I wished in my future life and work.

Many strange machines filled the laboratory, all performing tasks that I could only guess at. But these machines were subordinate to the real science of this great room, being designed only to chemically and electronically nourish and develop the many human embryos that moved and grew in synthetically duplicated mother-blood in sealed bottles.

The older ones kicked and tugged healthily at the grafted umbilical tube which supplied the life fluid—called Icor, the "blood of the gods." And it was this blood that was the subject of the lecture the Titan now gave us.

He told us of the upkeep and preparation of this fluid, both in the embryo and the adult; the difficult and important part being (he now stressed his words with greater emphasis with his attention bent especially toward me) the process of detecting and removing the slightest trace of the radio-active poisons that cause age.

I studied and I learned! These were the processes which had given the planet Mu its health and enabled us to live under more aging suns than other races. These were the life methods that had given us our fecundity; which had populated space for thousands of centuries with the seed of Atlan. I wanted to know all there was to learn about them.

The Titan, an old master at this most basic process of Atlan life, had imbued me with an enthusiasm for the true creation of life in its infinite possibilities of growth—such as no mere painter ever had. The delicate handling of those ultra-minute products of disintegrance from which primary integrations are formed; the mixing of these integrations into the atoms of elements; the chemistry of combining these atoms into the molecules of the substances used in the manufacture of the synthetic blood, Icor—all these steps were sheer artistry, yet were made as simple as child thought by the genius of the Titan.

Once more the Titan commented on the proposed emigration from Mu, weaving it into his lecture. There seemed to me to be an undercurrent of double meaning in his motive for repeating it; a double meaning that I strove to associate mentally with the fear-thing that was something else and also something so secret it must not be mentioned. It was as though even the fact that there was fear of that "something" must be kept secret. Our aging sun (he said) threw off increasingly large amounts of these sun's seeds, small but dense and active disintegrative particles, and I learned that keeping Atlan's peoples young was an increasingly difficult job for the technicons. I learned that the coordinators and rodite [14] were preparing the plans and ships for our migration to a young, new-born sun, where the force setup of life conditions left a greater margin of exd for intake of power, where integrance went on at a faster pace, and where the infection that caused the occasional trouble with detrimental energy robotism or detrimental err [15] in the human did not occur.

When the lecture in the embryo laboratory was finished we filed back to the classroom, and there the Titan flipped the switch that controlled the teleyes that supplied the home telesets of many with the course. We had not been dismissed, and I could see from the puzzled looks on the faces of the other students that this was not in accordance with the regular schedule.

For a long moment the Titan looked at us, and especially at me. Then he spoke:

"Today things have been said and seen and discussed in this class that had no direct bearing on the course you came here to take. You, Mutan Mion, have been the most brash—" my face grew red, and he hastened to add, "No, Mutan, I do not mean that you have been too forward; I meant brash in the sense that you have exposed yourself to a greater danger than that of my wrath." His eyes twinkled at the word wrath, and I knew that such would never be much of a danger! "I meant the menace that has caused the fear you have somehow seen in me. Perhaps you have sensed this in other places in Tean City, among others of the Titans; so it must be, for you to have been so certain of it as to challenge me.

"Yes, there was, and is, fear in me. And it is a fear that we all try to keep secret because those of us who show fear also show suspicion if not knowledge, and either has been equivalent to the signing of a death warrant. There are spying rays on us . . . at the moment we are screened . . . that seek out our knowledge and destroy us before we can coordinate it into an effective counteraction to the thing that is going on; to the thing we fear."

"What is that thing?" I breathed aloud, so intense was my interest.

The Titan drew a deep breath. "It has come to me that certain groups of Atlan are against the projected migration, and the recent disappearance of several men important to our work lends color to the story. Of course we all know that the only units able to do anything of the kind would be the key rodite of Sub Atlan and Center Mu. Some of these may have accidentally suffered a severe flashback of detrimental ion flow, so that their will has become one under detrimental hypnosis. What rodite area has become so corrupt as to allow such a condition to go unchecked I cannot understand; but that we are all in danger until the thing is checked is most certainly true.

"Therefore, since you here have gained an inkling of something wrong, it is only your right to be aware of it, so that inadvertent words may not cause you great harm. Also, we must fight this thing; and all of us must fight. So you may consider yourselves deputized by the ruling life of Mu to seek out the information that will clear the way for the migration. Until that is done we suffer fear, not new to me, but new to most of you.

"You may go."

Looking back at his gigantic form as I left the classroom, I saw him musing deeply; and the concern on his face told be that things must be even more fearful of consequence than he had made us believe. Reason told me, too, that it must be so—for great indeed must be the evil that can bring fear to the heart of a Titan, the super being of all Mu and of the universe.

Footnotes

12   Ter—the Lemurian word for cold.—Ed.

13   Impressed with the implications contained in this portion of the story of Mutan Mion, we wrote Mr. Shaver for additional information on this theory of the cause of age. This information is curious, because some of the theories seem to be modern (by Mr. Shaver) and others those of Mutan Mion, with no particular designation as to which is which. However, we present the whole for your judgment.

"The sun itself seems to be the mother source of all radioactivity, infecting all the earth's surface and all the life on its surface. The sun projects minute disintegrances down upon us in a steady, numerous rain whose effects we call age. In water the poison is heavily present in suspension, especially so in thermal springs. In the air the poison floats forever with the tiny thistledown of dust it has infected and to which it clings. It settles on the leaves of plants. So we take the poison in with every breath, with every bite of food, with every drink of water; thus we age as the poison accumulates.

"But we do not have to let in that poison; we can protect ourselves and grow through a longer youth to a much greater age, with superior mental powers. It is very plain that a mother's body cells, although replaced every four to seven years, are not young because they remain in contact with the poison retaining fabric of the body and so age swiftly. Yet, the baby is young. Young because it gets filtered blood, filtered through the placenta—and would remain young if the poisons were to be continued to be filtered out by a duplication of the placenta filter. The stalk of a plant is old, yet its seed is young, capable of reproducing itself without passing on the poisons of age. It is because the stalk contains a filter to prevent passage of the poison to the seed. The simple filtration processes of birth and seeding CAN BE COPIED by man, thus putting off old age.

"Here are a few verbatim quotations from Madame Curie's notes: 'Finally, the radiation of radium was contagious. Contagious like a disease and like persistent scent. It was impossible for an object, a plant, an animal or a person to be left near a table of radium without it immediately acquiring radioactivity—becoming radioactive—a notable activity which a sensitive apparatus could detect.' A later page: 'Thus the radio elements formed strange and cruel families in which each member was created by degeneration from the mother substance—radium was created by degeneration from uranium—polonium from radium, etc.' And from a later page: 'When one studies strongly radioactive substances special precautions must be taken if one wishes to be able to take delicate measurements. The various objects used in a chemical laboratory and those used in physics experiments all become radioactive in a short time, and affect photo paper through black paper. Dust, the air of the room, one's clothes all become radio-active. The evil has reached an acute stage in our laboratory.'

"Note the word mother. The sun is the mother source of radioactives.

"It is a matter of common knowledge that certain watch factories formerly allowed workers (young girls of twenty) to tongue-tip the brushes with which they painted the radioactive dials. They died of OLD AGE at twenty and twenty-five years! Not of a disease, but of age poison; radioactive particles, whose origination is from the disintegration of the heavy metals of which radium is a member!"—Ed.

14 Rodite—Life pattern synchronizers.—Ed.

15 This is mainly due (explains Mr. Shaver) to depolarization of the matter of the brain; it is no longer earth polared, it is sun polared—and hence inducts the disintegrant flows from the sun into the brain by simple dynamic induction. I think a magnet could be sun polared and point to the poles of the sun just as an ordinary compass points to the poles of the earth. This is what happens to parts of the brain; they become sun polared. In the desert this is known as "cafard," to become crazed and kill until killed. Others are just stupid, depending on what parts of the brain are affected. The Malay

"amok" and the Norse "berserk" are the same phenomena. When it lies in the part of the brain devoted to memory, the result is absent mindedness. When it lies in the nervous system and ego recognition of activating centers, the victim is a killer or a repressive reactionary. It is simply true that man is an electrical machine which functions well when his energy flows are of his own creating, but functions especially ill when the energy flows are from the sun.

The sun is quite a dynamo; it always gives off, from the surface; while earth always takes in, from the surface. Much of this intake is "snap-back"; that is, it is returning to a state of matter. Gravity is merely the disintegrant energy of suns returning to material form. Much of it, however, is like radium, a persistent disintegrant seed of a sun. Radioactivity is the seeds of disintegration.

Hence, a mind powered by sun particle energy flows of a detrimental nature becomes robot. The result is robotism, or the inability to think constructively. Victims of detrimental err have but one basic thought, to kill, in keeping with the natural elemental instinct of the disintegrant metals. (The reader has been presented here with two sensational theories which appear in complete form later in the manuscript; the nature of gravity, and the interrelation of energy and matter in an endless circle.—Ed.

CHAPTER III.

TERROR IN TEAN CITY

That evening Arl took me to a dance. Never had I known that there could be such pleasure! And as a part of it all I discovered that my education was to continue through every waking hour, whether in scheduled class or not. There was so much to be learned from actual living! And Arl, it seemed, was determined that nothing should be lacking in my education. Nor did I object, for nothing suited me better than to have her, beautiful tail and all, showing her friendship and interest.

The dance, she told me on the way to the hall in a rollat car, was very scientifically handled by trained technicons. The stimulation of human attraction between male and female, she told me, was due to the generation of many kinds of tiny and fecund spores which grow and are released upon stimulus by male and female. The male spores grow in the female and vice versa, just as pollen between flowers. This cell pollen and the sensation of its growing presence is love. I could imagine the immense fecundity given this process by the strength of the Atlan race, whose growth and youth [16] never cease.

We arrived at the place where the dance was to be held, and I found a great room, tastefully draped, and decorated by paintings that depicted such scenes of love and joy and health as I have never before seen. Just as the paintings at the Hall of Symbols held forth that invitation to join in the elevation of the race, so did these paintings show the way to participation in love and joy.

The dance had already begun and we joined the throng on the floor. Almost instantly I was aware of the influence of stimulating electromagnetic frequencies. I felt the flow of exd of appropriate attunements; my nerve cells responded in a thrilling fashion.

The stimulating rays strongly ionized the air of the hall; making it extremely conductive to the electric pressure of the body aura, so that the dancers were intensely aware of each other. The consequently augmented vital aura of the cell pollen permeated the hall. It was absorbed by my body, and by that of lovely, faun-legged Arl snuggled in my arms, and by all the young, ecstatic bodies of those who danced about us. Under the stimulus, we wove intricate patterns on the gleaming floor; and the odor music of the Atlans wove into the sound music many scent accompaniments. These scents are of the most penetrative and nutrient of all the food chemicals, feeding the nerves as they are driven into the body by strong sound waves of a penetrative frequency.

In the enhanced delight of the dance I was oblivious of all but the bundle of vitality to which my pulse and soul were synchronized, and my arms held Arl as a treasure beyond value.

Then, as I lost myself in pleasure, it happened. The madness of the fear that was upon Tean City struck; and for the first time in my life I knew the true meaning of terror!

Arl screamed, and pushing me from her, pointed to the edge of the dance floor. There the great shoulders of a horned son of a Titan hunched, one big hand clutching in desperate agony at the folds of a drape, the other pointing up and out to indicate the path of the ray that played upon him. Even in the face of death his only thought was to tell what he knew of the fear; and to point out its direction so that the technicons might answer with a ray of their own.

But nothing checked the ray; and I realized that contrary to all the usual rules there was no guard ray on duty. No wonder there was fear in Atlan! Slowly the huge youth's face turned black, his legs buckled, he fell and rolled over on his back, tongue protruding and eyes staring. He was dead.

His friends rushed to him, but the deadly ray had not ceased. It played first on one figure and then on another; each victim rolling in turn to the floor, face black with death.

"By the Elder Gods!" I swore to myself at the realization that no guard ray was going to protect us. "It is true; our perfect government is not so perfect after all!"

I stood as though oblivious to the fact that death might strike my way too. I could only look and rage within me at the death that played about the recently joy-filled hall. Within me the stimulating rays still caused an elation, but it was submerged beneath the surge of wrath that made my blood hot.

Arl was tugging at my elbow, the canny will to live of the female evident on her face in an expression of anxiety and calculation. Together we left the hall, taking a route along which her clicking hooves led me. We kept with a group of young Atlans who walked, without panic or the impulse to run, toward the parked rollats. I knew why; they feared to attract a spy-ray to themselves.

Arl's fingers pressed warningly on my arm, and I heard her whisper, her voice low, casual. An excited tone might have attracted the curiosity of the mad mind behind the black deaths, who must even now be surveying the scene of his mad acts of killing in grisly satisfaction.

"Listen to that man just behind us—"

I listened. His voice was also casual—held no excited note. In his voice was the cultured note that was evidence of one who has absorbed much of the vast education obtainable in Tean City.—"also heard that what lies behind the fear and death here is the mad wish of certain rodite to appropriate the whole fleet of ships prepared for the migration and go to the new sun leaving nothing behind alive with brains enough to build and fly ships in pursuit. Thus they would have the new sun's clean light entirely for themselves and their future seed."

A selfish thing, indeed! But more mad than selfish. Such a view could only be the result of detrimental err.

The speaker went on. "We, the mediocro, know how fecund life can be, but we also know the madness of refusing all of the normal units of life's fabric the right to existence and growth. No social fabric can be built of dull and lifeless robots which are so besotted with detrimental energy that they refuse the least of the units of the fabric their right to growth and intelligence. Therein lies the strength of the social fabric—the unit's realization of its own self and its place in the whole. The whole basis of a fuller life is the acquisition by mutual effort, the backing on which is woven the social pattern of the fabric itself."

I heard another voice, answering in agreement, yet with a troubled note evident in its tones, as if the speaker felt that agreement alone was not enough; that simply denouncing a thing that was as evil as this would not be enough. "Yes, this murderous effort is doomed to failure. The intelligent members of the guilty rodite must realize that such murder of the normal life unit is the refusal of their own right to share in the fruits of the social project. They must realize that such men as the Titan youth they killed have a potential value as great as their own."

Another voice chimed in. "Then why is it refused recognition? If they are intelligent, then why do they act so detrimentally? It must occur to them soon, or it will be too late."

"Unless they are all mad," said the first speaker. "The sane unit of such a project will see that the basic unit right is inherent to their own success, and realize that destroying those rights will wreck their own plans. The only thing it can he is the explanation a Titan growth technicon offered—that some rodite have been detrimentally charged by disintegrant coil leaks . . ."

I could not help breaking into the conversation.

"That is right! The thing has been explained to me that way; as a detrimental hypnosis in which the ego—or self-will—the self recognition of the mind centers confuses its self-originated impulses with the exterior-originated detrimental impulses to destroy. Such a condition is called dero, [17] or detrimental energy robotism. The thing is simple enough, but I cannot understand how it could happen here in Tean City, where perfection in romantics is so old. Such an occurrence is guarded against by many battle ro, by great organic battery brains raised for just that purpose. How could it happen?"

The two Titans looked at me and shook their heads. They knew as little as I how it could be.

"Well, it couldn't, but it did!" Arl said with feminine logic, and taking me by the arm, led the way to a rollat. In a moment we were speeding away from the dangerous area. Beside me Arl relaxed with a sigh, and I felt her trembling with reaction.

I put an arm around her. "Brave girl," I whispered.

We were soon nearing Arl's apartment, and looking down at her fresh, young face, I felt a wave of worry pass through me.

"I wish we were under that new sun right now; on those fresh-born planets of life with clean new coordinating mechanisms under rodite we ourselves selected and could therefore trust. I fear that the migration has been too long delayed—the old sun's disintegrant pressure upon the unseen base of our life is now too great for anything else to happen than what happened tonight. Can we help to strive against this immense err, deep-seated in the control minds about us as it must be; or must we flee at once, before they make impossible our flight, thinking of it has a danger of tale bearing?"

But Arl's lips were on mine as the rollat slowed before her home, an effective quietus to my dangerous words, and my mind no longer dwelt on the fear—nor imagined the embrace of a six-armed giant Sybyl female or the crushing coils of a snake woman about me!—for it was too busy recording the ecstatic sensations of the intense vital charge the faun-legged girl threw into her embrace. My mind gave up its worry in Arl's soft contact.

The next day I entered the classroom and found it empty. I went to the incubation laboratory and found several other early students standing there in silent consternation, the fear welling up almost to openness in their eyes. The Titan was not present, nor were any of his attendants. Some of the embryos were dead, others half-smothered; because no attendant had turned on the filtered, enriched air tanks which kept their nutrient fluid supply aerated. I started toward them, but a young son of a Titan stopped me.

"I turned them on," he said in low, evenly-measured tones.

"Where is the Titan?" I asked.

"No one knows," was the answer I got from all.

Other students came in now, among them Arl. She came to my side, but remained silent, troubled.

We waited a short time. Then a student called tutor center, to inquire. He turned to us with a peculiar look in his eyes.

"They say he is ill!"

"Ill?" The exclaimed question burst from all of us. In Atlan this was startling. Illness is almost unheard of; a rarity existent only on the space frontiers where new varieties of germs were sometimes troublesome.

The news brought Arl close to me, her silky-furred tail trembling as shudders shook her slim body. "Mutan, I am afraid," she whispered.

Her fear transmitted itself to me, and the thought came into my mind that this room was not safe. The same thought obviously had come to the others, because our movement toward the exit was as though by mutual accord. There was obviously some awful connection between the black deaths and the Titan's strange non-appearance. Yesterday the Titan had said a guard ray was on while he spoke to us so gravely of the fear—Had that guard ray been no guard at all? Had those evil rodite penetrated the guard ray, heard his words, known the Titan as a menace to their plan?

The class was dismissed—this time by fear!

And somehow I knew that the thought in my mind was in the mind of all. We had the same knowledge the Titan had. We were in the same danger. We were marked for disappearance, illness, or the black death! We must flee, now or never!

Proof of the thoughts of the others came almost instantly. As we trooped in assumed light-heartedness down the tunnel toward the rollat ways one, of the accompanying youths proposed a picnic in the forest to celebrate the unexpected holiday. He said it loudly in a gay voice, and the others chorused their delighted approval, a delight that Arl and I feigned too. All fell in with the project, the unspoken desire to flee the city strong in our breasts, our anticipation of being together among the trees, which subterranean dwellers seldom see, strong too.

I raced ahead with Arl, shouting gaily, "Let me lead you to the elevators." There was meaning in my voice, and intent in my mind. I was not forgetting my promise to my friend, the control-man.

We reached the shaft that led to Sub Atlan, from which we would take another lift to surface Mu. There, as we shot upward, I whispered the news to the control-man. "The terror is loose in Tean City," I concluded. "Escape as soon as you can. If at all possible, beg off from another descent and be away. There is great danger for all whom they suspect are aware of them."

He retained a straight face, but I could see the concern in his eyes, and the determination to make good his escape also.

As we lolled in apparent ease on the soft sod of the culture forest, the traditional empty glass made its appearance in the circle. No one spoke of it, but its significant reminder of death's clutch was a constant thing in my mind. Never had fear and death been a part of my thought before; but that empty goblet with its sweetly spiraling stem uppermost was no longer just tradition, but now had a meaning almost immense. What to do to avoid that damnable mechanical play of detrimental force from the mind of some unknown rodite, staring through the viewplates of his defective, detrimentally hypnotic mechanism, seeking to destroy the best first? [18] If they thought we were escaping they would seek us out and snatch us back.

I sat and mused. "Simple magnetics; yet such mighty minds as the Atlans fall before it. We must be clever . . ." I went on thinking of it; but again recurred the regret of last night. If only the migration had taken place a few years ago! But perhaps it had been so planned; and delayed? Delayed by the black death which had thus far struck so secretly and silently. The plan of the rodite must be near completion or their secrecy would have been maintained.

And then, as I sat there, an idea presented itself. I knew a way to escape, and I spoke quickly before my thoughts were clear enough for any unseen listener to read "Let us all charter a space ship and take a look at Mother Mu from above! There is no greater thrill than that to cap the day!"

As one we leaped to our feet. I knew then that our thoughts had been very similar; I had only been the first to express the next step in spoken words.

"We will have to take a shuttle ship first," said a young Titan quickly. "Come, I know the way."

Footnotes

16   The Atlans, Mr. Shaver reveals, were ever youthful, and never ceased growing. There was no such thing as "maturity" in the sense that growth stopped. Thus, an Atlan's age could be determined to a certain extent by his size. Many of them reached tremendous stature, sometimes as much as 300 feet, and heights of 40 feet and more were rather common. Mr. Shaver refers to "ancient" books which have been destroyed, which contained a great deal of Atlan knowledge and history, but points to references in the Bible such as "In those days there were giants in the Earth" as actual truth, recorded memory of the Titans. Especially significant is the definite statement "in the Earth" and not on it! The Atlans, by the use of their wonderful machines. kept their bodies constantly supplied with a sufficient amount of exd (the energy ash from which all matter is formed by condensation] so that their growth never stopped, but their bodies grew ever larger and heavier. Health itself was determined by weight; a healthy person was heavy. If he became ill,

he lost weight. Illness is the inability of the body to fully utilize the available exd, or is the result of an insufficient quantity of exd.—Ed.

17 Pressed for a more complete explanation, Mr. Shaver has defined "dero' for us:

"Long ago it happened that certain (underground) cities were abandoned and into those cities stole many mild mortals to live, At first they were normal people, though on a lower intelligence plane; and ignorant due to lack of proper education. It was inevitable that certain inhabitants of the culture forests lose themselves and escape proper development; and some of them are of faulty development. But due to their improper handling of the life-force and ray apparatus in the abandoned cities, these apparatii became harmful in effect. They simply did not realize that the ray filters of the ray mechanisms must be changed and much of the conductive metal renewed regularly. If such renewals are not made, the apparatus collects in itself—in its metal—a disintegrant particle which gradually turns its beneficial qualities into strangely harmful ones.

"These ignorant people learned to play with these things, but not to renew them; so gradually they were mentally impregnated with the persistently disintegrative particles. This habituates the creature's mind, its mental movements, to being overwhelmed by detrimental, evil force flows which in time produce a creature whose every reaction in thought is dominated by a detrimental will. So it is that these wild people, living in the same rooms with degenerating force generators, in time become dero, which is short for detrimental energy robot.

"When this process has gone on long enough, a race of dero is produced whose every thought movement is concluded with the decision to kill. They will instantly kill or torture anyone whom they contact unless they are extremely familiar with them and fear them. That is why they do not instantly kill each other—because, being raised together, the part of their brain that functions has learned very early to recognize as friend or heartily to fear the members of their own group. They recognize no other living thing as friend; to a dero all new things are enemy.

"To define: A dero is a man who responds mentally to dis impulse more readily than to his own impulses. When a dero has used old. defective apparatus full of dis particle accumulations, they become so degenerate that they are able to think only when a machine is operating and they are using it; otherwise they are idiot. When they reach this stage they are known as 'ray' (A Lemurian word not to be confused with ray as it is used in English.) Translated, ray means 'dangerous or detrimental energy animal.' Ray is also used to mean a soldier—one of those who handles beam weapons (note how the ancient meaning has come into our modern word)."—Ed.

18 Just as lightning strikes the highest point, so does detrimental force seek the most active and the healthiest fruit first—they are most attractive. The detrimental is only a film over an integrative ion which is attracted first to the most integrant bodies near. This holds true in thought movements also—thus a dero strikes at the best first.—Ed.

CHAPTER IV.

ESCAPE INTO SPACE

Accustomed as I had become to variform life, we presented a strange, almost fearsome appearing company to my eyes as we made our way toward the shuttle ship station. There was young Halftan, of Venusian blood, long-legged, web-footed and fingered, his eyes huge and faceted; his mate, a girl of Mu except that some forebear had given the line four arms, probably under the stimulus of mutation rays because the family pursuit of making instruments was one where twice the number of fingers could well be used; Horton, a young fellow of mixed bloods, older than the rest of us, quiet, but long-eared and sharp-nosed—a listening fox; his girl, a thin, gray, transparent-skinned maid of Mars, fragile and lovely, her large, leaf-green eyes lighting devoted friendship wherever they rested; two young Titan sisters, their horns just sprouting from under their curls, their great bodies new-budding into womanhood; their two escorts, of the Elder's special creation, large-headed youths of tremendous intelligence, their hands double-length, their necks and shoulders by far stronger than normal to carry their great heads easily, and finally a young Titan male, accompanied by his friend who was a distant cousin of my own Arl and whose sprightly, colorful femininity hinted that Arl's family must be especially noted for their beauty.

Together we made up a company of twelve life-forms of great diversity; and yet all of us citizens of Atlan; citizens apparently on an outing, now bound for a gay adventure to end a holiday's festivities in the supreme thrill, a sightseeing trip into space.

We dared not think of our true purpose; and I knew that at least the two Elder escorts were aware of what had brewed in my mind and would back me up when the time came. We thought only of our coming adventure, and tried to feel the delight of it so that even our emotions would register true to any spying teleray that sought us out to check on our motives.

The shuttle ship we boarded was a small, bullet-shaped plane containing little but a cabin, air-making equipment and a small fuel compartment in the rear. This plane was not a space ship, but only a sort of bullet to be shot from the surface of Mu to the large station ship of great weight which circled in its own orbit, just as the moon circles the earth forever.

To get the shuttle ship on its way gravity was neutralized by an upward beam of semi-penetrative force traveling at light speed which was turned on gradually until the car just floated in its cradle under the effect of the reverse friction to gravity of the force blast passing through the car. [19]

When the weight of the car was thus reduced to less than a pound, I turned on the rocket blasts very gradually and traveled up the reverse gravity beam by instrument. In thirty minutes we were circling the huge station ship as though we were in our turn its satellite just as it was a satellite of earth. With vernier rocket blasts, about the size of toy pistol explosions, the nearly weightless plane approached a landing. Above us spread the world we had just left, making an imposing sight as we settled into a cradle atop the space station.

When we stepped from the shuttle ship at the edge of the oval landing area, we saw several globe-bodied moon-men bustling about their own type of shuttle plane, a long, wingless splinter constructed of a very fragile and glass-like substance. Although I feared to think upon it, the moon was my next destination. One thing that all of us knew was that we never intended to return to earth. The blackened face of that son of the Titans, the noblest blood in Tean City, as he lay dying on the dance floor rose before me to tell me flight was not only best, but the only course for us.

In spite of myself my eyes roved over the black dome of space, searching for the lights that might indicate a pursuing craft. It seemed almost impossible that we were fooling the mad rodite and their spying telepath rays. In spite of all self-imposed mental guards, my mind seemed intent on shrieking "Escape! Escape!" through every possible loophole in my concentration.

I engaged the gnome-like moon-men in conversation in an attempt to still further blanket my turbulent mind. Arl caught my eye and wagged her tail in cheerful encouragement, seeming to divine what was on my mind. How expressive that beautiful tail of hers was; how much it could say; and with no dangerous thought waves to betray its meaning to those who must not receive on their sensitive instruments. With that tail, no language, no thought-transference was needed!

But even if pursuit developed, I had one trick up my sleeve. I dared not think of it, or some watching rodite informer might advise any pursuers of my plans and a way to circumvent them would be devised.

It struck me that not all of the rodite might know of recent conditions and developments in Tean City. Nothing had been announced on the tele-screen news. Thus, while we were escaping, others ought to know the truth, and certainly not all the rodite were dis-infected. They would not report what they read in my mind, and the rodite who knew would not attach special significance to others who knew; and the very fact that it was thought about in an unguarded way might cause them to dismiss us as of immediate danger, and thus blanket our intent to escape.

I thought of the dance, of the sudden striking of the black death on the dance floor, of my puzzlement as to what it might mean. I thought of the disappearance of our tutor technicon, wondered if he too were murdered. Any sub-rodite, getting a register of my thoughts, would certainly ponder the meaning of the unbelievable existence in center Mu of murder; murder whose actuality he could not doubt, because it would come to him as the unguarded and therefore true thought of a ro such as I was.

In double-quick time, still acting out our enthusiasm for an unexpected holiday, we chartered a fast space ship for an hour's time. An attendant led us to a cradle on the landing stage; and we entered the ship gaily.

The speedster rose slowly up the lifter beam under my control and when it was clear of the station ship I sent it hurtling outward.

When we were well out of sight of the station ship and picking up speed toward the moon I gave up thinking of our trip as a sight-seeing outing which was to proceed only a little way into space and then return, but began to think of the moon as our destination, meanwhile setting the autopilot destination needle on Venus. Then I pulled the throttle back to full on.

If what we had heard of the black death were true, it might well be that no space ships were allowed to leave the vicinity of Mu at all. Just the mere fact that we were hurtling straight away might have placed even more suspicion on our purpose if we maintained our original thought-fabrication. With the moon now our revealed destination, our true purpose was still veiled.

I switched on the electrically magnifying scope screen to the rear to look for possible pursuit. The scope had a screen of microscopic photo-cells which turned the tiniest light ray into an electrical impulse which was greatly augmented by vacuum tubes and the resulting impulse made a much larger cell on a viewplate glow strongly, giving a vivid image in half-tone.

Far behind us a craft sped along. Was it in pursuit? I watched it for long minutes, but there was no way of telling. It maintained its distance and its course. In a very short time their instruments could check our course, and if they were pursuing us, they would be unable to correlate it with my mental image of the moon as our destination; and they would be after us instantly. If they were merely harmless travelers to Venus, there would be no questioning of our own course.

I gave them time to check us with instruments, then I set the course pointer on Mercury, a planet almost never visited, and watched closely. The strange craft veered.

"They are on our trail," I said. The words broke a silence that had become almost intense.

Arl's cousin looked shocked. "Then we can't escape," she said. "They have a mechanical advantage over us."

One of the big-heads was eyeing me shrewdly "You have a plan," he said. It was a plain statement of fact, not a question. It was as though he did not ask what was my plan, but expected me to put one into operation now that the crucial moment had come.

"Yes," I agreed. "Now is the time to play my one card. I hope that it will be an ace."

"We have not asked nor even wondered about your plan once we observed that you had one," said the other big-head. "But now the time for secrecy is at an end. It is unnecessary. If we cannot escape, our intent to do so will be useless to hide; if we can escape, our intent will not need to be hidden."

"True enough. And I will be more than glad to relieve my mind of the strain of withholding what is in it," I said. "I am but a ro youth, and the task has been hard."

"But one that you have done well," observed the young Titan gravely.

I accepted the compliment with a thrill of pride. Praise from a Titan was something to which I was not accustomed—indeed, old Artan Gro had many times given me exactly the opposite.

"It is a matter of mechanics," I explained. "And the one thing I will be forced to blank out of your mind as I do it. I warn you all not to think on the matter when you see it performed. As to my plan of escape—I have an even greater one. I will explain fully in a very short while—we will go to one of the sunless Elder stations on a cold planet. The nearest of these is Quanto, on the very rim of this solar system."

"A good choice," approved the big-heads. "But one that rouses our curiosity in your 'mechanical trick' to a high pitch. Obviously you know that Quanto is seventeen and one-third billion miles away." [20]

I could almost read their minds. "Yes. Weeks away at the speed of this ship—and we have no food."

Even Arl's tail stopped wagging at that—but only momentarily. In her eyes I read that confidence I knew she had in me; a confidence that she herself felt was justified.

"Your plan!" she reminded me. "Now we know you have a definite one, for if you are aware of the fact that we have no food you must also be aware of a way to reach Quanto without it."

"Such great faith must be well placed," murmured one of the Titan maids. "I, too, can have no fear now that you have a plan."

I proceeded now about the thing I had in mind, taking care not to think of what I was doing, but think, rather of the appearance of my hands as they worked, of the movements of my knuckles, of the muscles that caused those movements, of the nerves that carried the message to the muscles . . .

It was a good thing for me now that I had listened so worshipfully to space pilots when I was younger; some of their adventures were going to stand me in good use. Autopilot mechanisms on these space ships were adjusted to a fool-proof speed, so that no speed-mad citizen could wreck a shipload of people. There was a stiff spring on the throttle, just a little stronger than a man's arm, which held the fuel flow to a safe maximum.

I found the case of the auto pilot locked and the key was naturally not aboard the ship, but kept by the attendant back at the satellite ship. But I found a way around that. I took the belts from several of my companions in spite of their puzzled faces and fastened them into one strong line. One end went around the throttle bar and with another I took a turn around a seat arm.

A dozen strong Atlan arms pulled the belt line taut at my bidding, and I took in all the slack at the seat arm. Back came the throttle bar. The acceleration of the ship spilled them all in a heap at the rear, but I held fast to the line and the bar stayed back.

Now our safety depended on whether the pursuing crew knew this simple trick—for many of the pleasure craft. which our pursuer plainly was, were as well powered as the police craft, although their autopilots restricted them to a much lower speed. If the pursuing craft's pilot did not think of adding other men's power to the strength of kis own hand on the throttle bar, he would never overtake me. Even police craft were set to less than maximum motive power, as the tubes burned out too quickly at full blast.

I watched the dark speck on the rear screen anxiously and slowly it grew smaller and smaller. When it had vanished the youthful Titan pounded me on the back until my ears rang and my knees buckled.

"You're a sly fellow, and your whole plan of escape is right. It's high time we ran away from the black death. I've worried and waited for it to strike me long enough. The Elder station on the cold planet are the best natured men you can find in space. Haven't been near a sun in centuries, and don't know the meaning of the word evil!"

He turned to the others and continued speaking eagerly. "They'll take us in, give us entrance cards to any government in space Personally I would choose some civilization that warms its cities with its own fires, and shuns all suns entirely. I've had enough worry waiting for Atlan's rulers to get wise to the danger and move. I want no more of these sun-bitten zany dero around me!"

The gray Martian maid spoke, her sensitive green eyes shining with admiration, her voice the slow singing speech of Mars "The best thing you did was not to tell us what you had in mind, for someone would have read our minds as surely as Venus loves us. We have lived in dread and indecision for many moons. The black death has struck day after day and no official word of it. No one can tell who is dead; there is no way to tell if anything is being done about the danger or not, for anyone who made the slightest effort to do so disappeared at once just as our loved teacher did. We all know that he was not ill; and we also all know that the day he made that announcement to us he had signed his own death warrant—but he had evidently decided he must, as no one else seemed to move. It has been terrible, and if you had planned this flight with us we would never have gotten away. We have been very lucky to get this far. Now, if you will take my advice, you will go at once far beyond any influence from Mother Mu's rodite, under another space-group of planets, and there we will learn how to live where such things as the black death do not exist."

The smile she bestowed on me was Martian magic.

It must have been the look on my face that prevented any further remarks by my companions, and caused them to look at me in new curiosity. If so, my next words fanned the flame of that curiosity.

"I spoke of a greater plan, a few moments ago," I said. "And I am afraid it does not call for such conclusions as you two have made. I am sorry, but neither of you have given me any advice that I like, as sound as it may seem."

"Speak on," prodded one of the big-heads, his eyes alight with interest.

I checked our course briefly to make sure we were headed for Quanto correctly before I answered him. Then I made myself comfortable in a cushioned seat and faced them.

"What is it that we have been fleeing?" I asked.

"Basically, an aging sun," said the young Titan reflectively. "The black death is merely a result of detrimental action on certain rodite who have become dero and even ray. We have fled from them, but the real cause of our flight is the sun."

"Do we flee as cowards, deserting our comrades?" I asked softly. "Or do we flee only that we may be able to make a new plan to take the place of the one that has been interrupted by the rodite dero?"

There was a wry smile on the face of the big-head. "The day has come," he said, "when I have seen a ro put a Titan to shame! Of course,

Mutan, we do not flee for cowardice, but to gain time and life to put up a fight. It is only that we have not thought it out as you have Nor has inspiration as yet given us such a plan."

"Then listen to mine," I said, "Just as it is with you, my first thoughts at realization of the fear that lay in Tean City were those of escape to a place where there was no fear. It is a natural reaction, especially if that possibility suddenly presents itself.

"Let us analyze the fear. First, the top unit of the force behind the black death must be a man in a very strong position, to stall off the whole migration as has obviously been done, and to control things so that no news leaks out about the terror that is otherwise so plain for many to see. So high and powerful must this man be that to fight against him on Mu itself must be to invite certain defeat. Perhaps even if we were to muster all clean-minded Atlans to the battle, we could meet only the same frustration as the migration plan has suffered—for is it not true that all Atlans who are aware of the danger of the sun's evil have made utmost effort to bring about the migration?"

"True enough," said a Titan maid. "No Titan has been unaware of the danger, and lately, even such ro as you have been brought into the plan. Perhaps it is fitting that the salvation of that plan come from the mind of a ro."

"Then here is the only salvation I can see," I said. "We must go to the Elders of Quanto. Through them we must contact the mightiest of the Titans and from them get advice and assistance. This thing may well become a space war before we are through—and as I see it, it must be so, or all the Atlans of Mu will be lost!"

I looked at Arl, to see if she listened, and she wagged her tail roguishly. Not only was she listening; she was thinking in tempo with me. At my glance her voice chimed in, doing things to my spine.

"Yes, and we ourselves must devote ourselves to the task, and go to a place where the growth rate is unlimited by law, so that we can become more equal to the job. It will take great power to displace the mad rodite.

On Quanto we must find some mighty and old and wise technicon to go along and assure us of a hearing; otherwise the power will not be given us. We need the very mightiest power the Elders of space can give us to save the people of Mu."

"If you but wag that tail of yours at them, Arl, they will give it to us!" I laughed because I could see in all those around me the same conviction and devotion to my plan that was in her. The youthful company laughed too. "Of that there can be no doubt," they agreed, whereupon Arl swished her tail before them and pirouetted about on her clicking hooves.

In that instant the fear was gone from our minds. Instead we were filled with gaiety and hope, and great determination to do all that lay in our power to end all fear.

We circled Mercury, straightening out on a direct path for Quanto, constantly accelerating until it was unnecessary to explain why lack of food did not worry me. The young Titan remarked: "We will be at Quanto within twenty-four hours. Already our speed is approaching that of light. [21] air locks. At last we were in the home of the kindly men from sunless Nor!

I leaned back with a sigh of thankfulness, feeling that I had saved at least some of the good life seed of ancient Atlan from the madness that was overtaking all of its races under the aging sun. To save still more would be a collossal effort; but as Arl's arms drew about my shoulders, I knew that such effort was worthwhile.

The purpose of life was plainer now. Such beauty and tenderness did not live in words or in paintings. Only in understanding and caring for the life seed, the bearers of future race growth, could a man find the true meaning of life. And in the mighty job that lay ahead in enlisting aid for the saving of our people from the black death of the mad rodite I knew I would become a man or die.

Footnotes

19 Mutan Mion explains that gravity is the friction of condensing exd, ex-disintegrance, falling through matter into earth. By using a beam of similarly condensing particles of ex-disintegrance a harmless beam of upward gravity is obtained which can levitate matter slowly or drive it upward at immense speed. All space is filled with the ash from disintegrance of the suns of the universe. This, condensing again into matter, is integrance or gravity.—Ed.

20 Mutan Mion says this is the eleventh and last planet of the solar system. The tenth (and yet undiscovered, though predicted by astronomers) is two billion miles beyond Pluto, which is itself nearly four billion miles from the sun.—Ed.

21 Mutan Mion, apparently, holds no brief for the "limit velocity" of light; or that the speed of light is the ultimate speed. According to Mr. Shaver's letters on the subject: "Light speed is due to 'escape velocity' on the sun, which is not large. This speed is a constant to our measurement because the friction of exd, which fills all space, holds down any increase unless there is more impetus. The escape velocity of light from a vaster sun than ours is higher, but once again exd slows the light speed down to its constant by friction, so that when it reaches the vicinity of our sun, no appreciable difference is to be noted. A body can travel at many times the exd constant, under additional impetus, such as rocket explosions. A ship whose weight is reduced to a very little by reverse gravity beam can attain a great speed with a very small rocket. Once beyond the limits of matter gravity ceases and the ship becomes weightless. Speeds over that of exd constant must be under constant impetus, for the friction slows them down quickly again, especially so in the case of solids. Sound, as an example, travels through air at a constant speed—and yet the impetus is obviously different in each case! The only conclusion is that the air itself is the governing factor in the speed of sound, which always remains appreciably the same. So it is with light. Both depend for their velocity on an initial impetus. Both remain constant because below a cerfain speed, friction disappears."

Your editors have been constantly amazed at the interchangeability of Mr. Shaver's (Mutan Mion's?) physical phenomena, or rather, their adaptability to one great physical law which we have as yet hardly begun to comprehend in its entirety. However, at this point a brief definition might aid the reader in understanding many things he has already read and will read in the following pages.

Matter in all the cosmos is constantly disintegrating and integrating. There is the natural parallel as to whether the hen or the egg came first—did the integration come first, or the disintegration? But that is the one and only unanswerable question in the whole theory. Exd is the ash (matter so finely divided as to become energy rather than matter) of disintegrating suns. It spreads out and fills all space. Then, perhaps because of the presence of an actual bit of matter (as in the case of the salt grain in the salt solution that commences precipitation which does not end until all the salt is once more in its original form), or under the influence of a magnetic field which draws the exd On Quanto, we knew, a group of Elder technicons from sunless Nor, a group of sunless planets 0.16 light years away, had lately established an observatory for the study of our planetary system. [22] It was these Elders I wished to contact in my effort to enlist aid for our cause.

Our trip to Quanto consumed slightly over twenty-four hours, the hunger of which we could easily endure; and on the landing station we switched to a shuttle ship.

As we settled into the cradles of the great cavern's entrance on Tiny Quanto, liquid air glistened over the view panes. The ship rocked as the cradle connected with its conveyor and was drawn by it into the cave through the together, integration commences and the exd once more becomes matter. This fall of exd and its condensation is what causes gravity. When Newton was hit on the head by an apple, it was by an apple that was pushed down upon his head, rather than pulled down; since gravity is the friction caused by the fall through matter already existent of condensing exd. Obviously a condensation is a falling together of a finely divided element into a grosser state.

There are many finer points, staggering in their implications, concerning this theory which are not necessary to the reader's understanding of this manuscript; but they are being prepared in a monograph which is to be submitted to scientific circles.—Ed.

[22] Quanto lies beyond the jurisdiction of Mu's government, which holds sway over all the planets of the solar system except this tiny world. Quanto is on the rim of Nor influence and is used by them as an observation station. Because of its small size, it is unimportant to the government of Mu.—Ed.

CHAPTER V.

THE PRINCESS VANUE

We found the typical welcome that all the great ones accord to visitors. Our party was courteously received by the attendants, and we were directed to the administrative offices with swift efficiency.

For me, this first visit to a world people by other than Atlans or Titans was one of the most interesting of my life; but I did not find it half as exciting as my first glimpse of Tean City had been. The men from sunless Nor were of an amazing blondness, for no light but of their own making had ever struck their skins. Their size, as did that of Titans and Atlans, varied with their age and with the age of the parent. Thus, a son of a man of a hundred years age would be three times the size of a son of a man of thirty. [23]

Further, the race from Nor, who are called Nortans, are a straight race of men. There had been no intermingling of races of other forms, not because it was forbidden, but because their technicons had not made the variform technique of breeding available to the public and without it all such intercourse is sterile. Perhaps they are right, although I see much beauty in variforms—especially in my own lovely and completely desirable Arl with her beautiful, expressive furry tail and her dainty, clicking hooves; certainly their race is beautiful and vital enough to please anyone.

All about the city of the Nortans it was evidenced by many wholly unfamiliar devices that the science of Nor had forged ahead of our own;

and as I looked about, I knew why. Here was none of the fear that had pervaded Tean City; nor was there any of the sun-poison to be a detriment to constructive thinking in even the slight degree that evidently has long deterred the technicons of Mu from full scientific advancement.

The thought of the fear brought the need for haste once more home to me as we walked through the city toward the administrative buildings. It was better to continue our flight than to remain long even here, I knew. So, to improve time, I kept running over in my mind the desperate plight of center Mu; the delaying of the migration to a newborn sun; the fear of pursuit that was still with us; for I knew that in that administrative building toward which we were headed some watchful Elder of Nor was most certainly taking thought record of our minds, to see if there were harm in us.

So, when we reached our destination, it instantly became evident that we would have little explaining left to do. And at the same time, another thing became evident to me that filled me with terror. Fear, again, in the one place where I had thought I would not find it!

A young lady of the snowskinned Nortan race glided toward me, her hand outstretched in greeting, her voice a soft bell of welcome for all of us.

"We have read your thoughts and understand what brings you here. Follow me now to the Princess Vanue, chief Elder, for an oral check; and forget your fear, for soon you will be going to where fear is not. Your message spells danger to us, as well as to your poor, helpless fellows in Mu." [24]

It had been the words "Princess Vanue, chief Elder" that had struck a new kind of fear into me. The chief Elders had been described to me in Tean City. They are the oldest of the race, and are given official power, according to the value of their achievements to the race. They are of both sexes, and have learned all there is to know of the secrets of growth; how to manufacture their own life-supporting essences, nutrients and beneficial vibrants. And on their ability to improve upon the standard nutrients of the people often depends their success. Thus, when a simple ro like myself comes near one of these Elders, his will becomes their will automatically; for it is overcome by the great, all-pervading force of the life within them. One hardly notices this when the Elder is of the same sex, but when that life force is of the opposite sex the attraction is so great as to be irresistible. So true is this that seldom is a ro of one sex allowed too near an Elder of the opposite sex; for never again would the poor ro free himself of love for the Elder.

My spirit trembled when I knew the Elder to which we were being taken was a woman; a woman who for unknown centuries had absorbed all the essences of growth-promoting substances. And too, Nor was a place where growth science must be far, far ahead of our own sun-baked sciencon's achievements. Never would I be able to free myself of the spell that woman-force would cast upon me!

I looked desperately at Arl's sweet face. Never again would I love her if this thing were true. In Arl's eyes I read the same fear, and I know then that she surely loved me and I was torn by the approaching loss. However, I dimly understood that it must be necessary—for no man near an Elder woman can deny her the truth of love for her.

We left the building and presently were ascending a long, transparent boarding tube into the side of a space liner that lay like a sleeping monster in the launching cradles. This was one ship that could land directly on a planet! But then, Quanto was small. We passed through a series of airlocks, reached the inside of the ship.

It was a long way into the center of the ship. As we progressed, I noted that all the ro who passed were maidens; beautiful white Nor maidens with glittering white-yellow hair that floated about their heads in a cloud, so fine was it that it was air-borne.

Soon I became aware of an aura of complementary forces that I knew came from the Nor Chief Elder, Vanue, whom we were undoubtedly now nearing. Her force scent grew stronger as we approached a mighty door set across a corridor. In glowing letters of hammered metal above this door was the legend:

VANUE
Elder Princess Of Van Of Nor
Chief Of Nor On Quanto

The great door, I discovered, was an airlock; to hold in the ionized and nutrient-saturated air of the chamber. These chambers the Elders seldom leave, since all evil is restrained from entering.

As we passed through the lock, the terrific stimulation of this conductive electrified medium seized us in a mighty ecstasy. We were drawn as by a powerful magnet toward a huge figure which was an intense concentration of all the vitally stimulating qualities that make beauty the sought-for thing that it is.

Within me I could feel the compass of my being swinging toward its new center of attraction. I was no longer myself. I was a part of that mighty being before me. My thought was her thought; I was her ro until she chose to release me.

Could she release me? I could not even wish it, nor ever would. Within me I knew that, and I felt no resentment, no regret—only joy.

All of eighty feet tall she must have been. She towered over our heads as she arose to greet us, a vast cloud of the glittering hair of the Nor women floating about her head, the sex aura a visible iridescence flashing about her form.

I yearned toward that vast beauty which was not hidden for in Nor it is considered impolite to conceal the body greatly, being an offense against art and friendship to take beauty out of life. I was impelled madly toward her until I fell on my knees before her, my hands outstretched to touch the gleaming, ultra-living flesh of her feet.

Beside me the other youths from center Mu were in the same condition of ecstatic desire.

As our hands touched her flesh, a terrific charge of body electric flowed into us. We fell face downward in unbearable pleasure on the floor.

She picked us up one by one and placed us on the desk before her. Waist-high now were our burning eyes. She bent to meet our gaze; and the mighty beauty of the eyes of the Elder princess of Nor flashed a question into our minds. As one man we chorused:

"Yes, it is true! Evil has the upper hand in center Mu; in Tean City itself!"

It was then that I realized how far ahead of Mother Mu's Titan and Atlan technicons were the Nortans and,

I supposed, all other great ones of the dark worlds. For Vanue wasted no more time on us, but bending toward the banks of instruments before her throne, pulled a lever and through all the ship was heard the warning signal of departure. As if they were my own, I knew her thoughts! Quanto was to be evacuated.

The Nortans were certainly not the sun-spoiled sleepyheads our own race had proved to be. She understood the awful danger that could threaten a planet's multitudes' under the thumb of the dero madness.

At her willed command we all ran to seats that circled the throne. They were mounted on acceleration absorbers. The grand hand pressed the bar that lifted the now weightless ship up the force beam flowing out of the cavern.

Even through the thick walls of the ship we heard the huge airlocks scream shut behind us. Then we were out in space headed toward Nor, the vast cold planet where this Elder Goddess' daughter had been born centuries before. I realized that our precipitate departure was sure evidence that our news had meant much more than nothing to Vanue. She had enough Elder God sense in her to know that flight was imperative. There were misgivings in my breast as I wondered if any Atlan Elders or rodite had knowledge of mighty Vanue's presence in Quanto. It might make a great difference if they did!

As the acceleration lessened toward the midpoint of our takeoff, freeing us from our seats, the whelming voice of the great woman-being swept us.

"You children will remain with me until your future is settled. I will thus be sure that you are fully rewarded for bringing us such vital information."

The soft, singing voice of the gray maid from Mars questioned her, and in its notes was gray also.

"Will you . . . can you . . . then give us back the love of our dear ones, which has cleaved to you?" There was a powerful pleading in her voice that penetrated even through the blanketing ecstasy that held me.

Infinite tenderness and compassion seemed to flow from the eyes of the great one.

"There is a way to do that," the master voice answered; and she bent swiftly toward the Mars maid, her great eyes flashing a strange thought I could not wholly read; a tender woman-language into the eyes of the Mars maid.

That simple Martian magic had made another friend, this time a great one indeed.

It was a strange passage. Most of it seemed more a dream than reality. Such things as the tremendous gait we built up—far more than light speed—and the great distances we traveled were the realities, but I barely noticed them. More real was the unreality of the thin, lovely forms of the Nor maids moving about their mighty princess, the soft fires of their floating hair like seedling flames from the vast fire of Vanue's god-life crowned by its floating cloud of yellow; our own eyes burning like the spotted wings of moths against the screen of her will; the sad faces of our own maids beside us, gazing first at the fierce white flame of her body and then at our own bemused selves; the vaulting of the vast ship walls about us; the unfamiliar instruments blinking and whirring.

It was a very real dream to me—a dream I knew I would never stop dreaming. Strange passage . . . Ever the whisper of the feet of the Nor maids on some swift errand; the soft rumble of the voice of their living Goddess and the answering bright song of her worshipping maidens. Yes, it was a strange passage, and every mile of it brought home a fascinating realization.

I had embarked on the most amazing voyage of my whole life. The very thought of what now certainly lay before me was enough to stun my mind into an apathy of thinking that was hard to overcome; yet my mind was so full of excitement that it did strive to think, to add to the realization of what the future would hold. A new life was at hand; opening to wonders that staggered me to think of them—and awed me into all-engulfing reverence.

To live to become what this Nor princess had become; to have the love of people as she had the love of these Nor maids—that is the real dream. I knew that I must gain the key to the door of a way of living that would lead to the full value of the Nortan life.

So it was, sitting in the thrall of that too-strong beauty of woman-life, we noted so little. How much time passed? I will never know. It was as if all body functions ceased, as though food and drink were not needed—as long as we were in the presence of Vanue of Nor. But I did know that she was in continual communication with the planet Nor over the space telescreens. Face after face appeared before her, murmured briefly and intensely, and vanished; only to be replaced by others. I knew vaguely that she was calling for a conference on the strength of our information; and sensed also that we would attend that conference at her side.

The thought dawned on me slowly. Here was an honor few ro ever attain in the first century of their growth. By old Mother Mu! To see those Elders of Nor, the whole lot of them, male and female, all at once . . . ! That would be more than one could well stand. An overpowering, devastating ecstasy . . .

Well, it would be an interesting death. [25]

Footnotes

23   Proportionately this would not be true. A man of a hundred considering he did not stop growing at the usual age, would certainly not be three times as large as at thirty. A baby doubles its weight in six months, doubles it again in eighteen. Thus the rate decreases in proportion to total mass, although the actual poundage increase is the same for a similar period of time. Later, however, this poundage begins to lessen until maturity is reached, where growth ceases altogether. In the time of Mutan Mion, however, growth was a constant thing, ended only by death. And the rate of growth could even be increased, if desired. This is what Arl was referring to when she mentioned that it would be necessary to "grow" to be able better to perform their mission. The reader will see the methods of this stimulated growth demonstrated further on in this manuscript.—Ed.

24   The Nortans, as did the Atlans and Titans, spoke the universal language of space; a language originated by a Titan Elder of the far past. The name of the language is Mantong. The original individual language of each race has fallen into disuse as the three racés have intermingled through all space. This is the same language of which the alphabetical key was published in the January 1944 issue of Amazing Stories, and also as an appendix to this book.—Ed.

25   This reference to death from mere association with the Elders is singularly intriguing. According to Mr. Shaver, the Titans, Atlans and Nortans had the ability to bestow beneficial forces upon less favored mortals, such as Mutan Mion (a ro), and also radiated a perpetual flow of life energy which was beyond their control to cut off from any ro who visited them. Hence, the animal magnetism of Vanue was such as to cause Mutan Mion's whole being to be drawn to her body with a force so great that it superseded any other love he might have had. Her attraction commanded all of his maleness, his ability and capacity for love of the opposite sex.

Now we find him referring to the possibilty of dying from too much of this animal magnetism. Obviously in his mind a superstition has been built up which has enhanced his imagination of the effects of meeting the Elders in a great group. He refers to meeting the Elders as being "a great honor" for ro less than a century old. Therefore we can discount his belief that it will be fatal to him; because it is sometimes done to ro younger than a century as an "honor" and without fatal result. The truly interesting factor here is when we consider Mr. Shaver's constant insistence that dark space is full of Titans, Atlans and Nor-tans, and that they do not visit our world because it is plagued by the sun's poisonous radioactives and is a cause of death. They shun their ancient home, Mu. We, says Shaver, are a quarantined people under an evil sun. We have no value to them. In their language we are errant (detrimental energy animals: E—energy; R—dangerous dis force; AN—animal; T—force of growth. Literally errants are animals whose force of growth is directed by a dangerous dis energy and is therefore evil). Can we assume that he is incorrect in his assumption that these super beings never visit the earth, and that such instances as the biblical references to angels, Christ, and other things are actual records of such visits? Perhaps it is significant that the reference to these things always seem to include effusion of an energy of some sort; i. e. the radiance of the angel who drove Adam and Eve from the Garden; the brilliant light that blinded Saul as he rode to destroy Christians; the radiance amidst which Elija, and Christ himself, ascended into Heaven; the light that came from the burning bush and the voice that spoke to Abraham.—Ed.

CHAPTER VI.

CONCLAVE OF THE ELDERS

I never knew how much time the voyage consumed; but it seemed very soon that the great vessel floated down the landing beam into the white and yawning face of a landing area on a station satellite of Nor while I and the other youths dreamed on almost oblivious in the quarters of Vanue.

Still in that dazed dream of love we followed among her maidens into the tubes and aboard the special shuttle ship awaiting her, and shot off to Nor looming not far away. We did not pause on Nor's dark surface, but descended into the depths of a great cave toward the council place somewhere in center Nor.

I had thought in the past that the Titans were mighty of thought and size—but what I saw now eclipsed anything I had ever heard of the glories of our own races. Big and vital as was Vanue, she was but a little child among the tremendous Nortan Elders and Gods.

There are no words to describe what the development of unchecked growth in man brings forth. These ancient Nor-tans, who had studied and purified all the source-substances of growth and combined them into an endless variety of nutrients which they introduced into their bodies by many means—borne in electric flows; on penetrative sound waves; by injections; by direct feeding—had been growing at a fierce rate for unknown centuries. Their inner beings had evolved in various ways, so that they were evidently of a more complex atomic and molecular construction than ordinary flesh. There is no way to describe the qualities of thought, of inner strength of spirit seen on their faces and in the aura that is always about such beings.

We trooped after Vanue as she entered the vast reaches of the council cavern and took her throne by the side of her father, a mighty bulk of man-flesh but only a lesser luminary in that gathering.

Before the council came to the business at hand we were treated to a brief prelude of entertainment—psychologically a reward for the effort of coming to the council. It vas a prelude to music and dancing, a review of the best talent of the planet, calculated to bring the minds of the council into harmony on the subject of the welfare and glory of the race. Entertainment, yes; but the amusements of Elder Gods are nothing to pass over.

What it all meant was beyond me; I was aware only of the awful beauty and tremendously fecund strength of the dancers—bred and fed by wizard technicons of growth; trained to express meaning and emotion of a kind too vast for ro to grasp. They danced in a vortex of conductive rays which carried their thought and body essence, augmented by apparatus, to each watcher.

The climax was the appearance of the greatest beauty of the planet—a sorceress of the art of entertainment named Hypaytee—who wore on her head a device which caused a vast augmentation of the thought images of her mind to play about her body in a tremendous revealment of the infinitely developed soul of woman. I had loved woman—hut never before had I undestood even vaguely what development did to the greatest value of life. The rewards this woman could give a man by the use of her mind alone, coupled as it was to that mighty, sinuous dancer's body expressing all the things that draw men to women, brought the concourse of Elders to their feet in an earth-shaking applause and a mighty vow to care for the race that produced her. This thought was also projected from the control rays which took root in every heart. It came to me, too: and I was a Nor-man now, no matter what I had been before!

Then Vanue's thought flashed out, setting the thought cloud [26] areas into coruscation with an alarm, a command to attention. I was brought out of my daze to see my own thought record projected in the thought clouds. I saw once again, as real as the first time I had seen it, the fear on the faces of the six-armed Sybyl of the Info screens; the striking of the black death at the dance; the hideous fear on the faces of the dancers; Arl's sweet face contorted in a scream.

A thought-record from the brain of each of our group from Tean City followed. It was evidence enough, thus gathered together, that evil had the upper hand in Mu.

My own efforts to conceal my thought as I planned our escape and the trick of the belts on the throttle that had resulted in our success finished the record display.

I was mightily surprised to hear applause and a great thunder of voices calling for me—Mutan Mion of Atlan. They called for me, the stupid artist! those vast voices from hundreds of ancient beings, some of them three hundred feet in height!

Vanue held me out in her two hands for all to see. And as I became the center of their attention, my embarrassment exceeded any emotion of a similar nature I had ever had. If I had known that they would think of an escape from such a condition as so much of a feat it is probable I would never have tried it. I would have been hopeless of success from the very inception of the fool-hardy thought.

I was put down again, my face red, my thoughts flustered, my embarrassment a flood of discomfort in me—but a discomfort that held within it a strange glow of humility that was at the same time a glow of pride. I was proud with a just pride; and I felt somehow that it was not my own pride, but the pride of Vanue, whose utter slave I had become. Vanue, Elder of Van of Nor, was proud of her ro!

The actual conference of the Godheads took place now in thought projections in the thought-cloud area. I saw that any thought, no matter how abstract, could be projected in these clouds by thought augmentors. [27] They used an image language instead of words, and their talk was to me but a whirlwind of changing forms, faces, geometrical figures, maps of space and figures on orbits and many other things incomprehensible to me and probably to most of the ro present. The powerful minds of the Nortans functioned too rapidly for us to grasp any but the simplest meaning in the ideographs unfolding in the cloud before us. But I did gather that some action was to take place at once to save the Atlans and the Titans of Atlan from the derodite.

Now from the mists of the Elder Gods' highest throne of all came a swift ray that lanced down and touched me delicately. An ecstasy of change came over me. What that ray did to me and told me in the next brief instant I can never say in any words. Then a voice spoke out:

"Muton Mion of Mu, we have seen the great compassion and love for your fellow man that lives in your breast. We admire such greatness in such a tiny ro; and because of the love of man in you we have decided that it must not go without full satisfaction in deed.

"You came here to gather together an expedition and return to Mu for the rescue of your comrades who are in deadly danger. Never could you carry such a gigantic project as this would require to its successful completion—and yet you have done it; for we of Nor have made a solemn vow to rescue the men of Atlan on Mu and to destroy the derodite who threaten to spread their evil even into dark space.

"However, because of your great desire, we have planned a place for you in this great mission. You shall have your part in it; and you shall have another duty which is worthy of your capacity for compassion. We, the Nortans, have seen in your mind a vision of the far future—of a time on Mu when men shall be slaves of the degenerate sun around which it circles; of a time when they will be but mentally deficient savages living out a life span compressed to an irreducible minimum by radioactives.

This may be a true vision, in part or in whole—for we may not succeed entirely in our mission. We may even fail!

"Therefore, we give to you the task of preparing a message, in great duplication, to these pitiful men of the future—so that there may be some hope that those among them who have the mental power to fight against their cruel environment may make their lives in some measure complete. This message will be left on Mu, and in it, in many places for future man to find."

The voice ceased. The conference was over.

Footnotes

26 Three dimensional pictures were formed by projection of the image into a mass of gases held by electric pressure in a cloud whose particles glowed in various colors according to the mental wavelength of the vibration field in which they floated. Ordinarily the cloud is opaque white, and when the thought-picture is projected into it by the Nortan mind, it becomes transparent except for the particles which form the image in full color. The command for attention causes the whole cloud to change color from milky white to flaming red.—Ed.

27 In a letter from Mr. Shaver, this reference to augmentors is explained in great detail. Says Mr. Shaver: "I refer you to a picture printed in many high school books of ancient history. It is from the 'Book of the Dead' a copy of which could be obtained in any large library from a book about the 'Book of the Dead.' This picture shows a scene which is called a picture of the Gods, and is in two sections. On the lower section the Gods are 'weighing the souls' our historians tell us. Actually it looks like a butcher buying a hybrid hog: half hog and half deer . . . the animal has a line around its middle as though it had been cut apart and sewn together again. It is evidence of the hybrid breeding of animals by the Atlans and Titans of Mu.

"Another picture shows a teacher seated before an instrument, and before the teacher, facing him, is a group of students each holding a smaller instrument. This is an actual pictographic representation of the thought augmentor and the focusing device used to pick up its waves.

"Still another instrument pictured in ancient Egyptian glyphs is the crook the Pharoahs always carry. Notice the bottom end has a clevis—with holes. I have seen such handles protruding from the ancient weapon-beam apparatus. It acts as a beam director, like the stick of an airplane; and if removed would have kept the apparatus from being used by anyone else. Why else the clevis on the bottom? The origin of scepters was this carrying of the control handle to keep others from using the dangerous apparatus while one was gone for a short time.

"Certainly the use of this apparatus was very general in ancient times among rulers for it gave them control of men's minds and its use was always secret among them."—Ed.

CHAPTER VII.

A WEDDING ON NOR

As we passed from the misty vastness of the council cavern Vanue turned to us of Atlan, trooping behind her, and said in a serious voice.

"It is law among Nortans that no service to the race goes unrewarded. Now there are certain things I plan for you which I cannot give you legally except you swear to serve me always as my loyal followers. Is there anything to keep you from that?" Her eyes searched us one by one.

The Mars maid answered, her eyes shining:

"There is only our oath to the state of Atlan, and the present evil conditions render that oath void."

Vanue went on: "I am only a young Elder; you might do better than to follow me—my fortune in the future is not wholly assured. You might do better!"

"You have honored us, Vanue," said the Mars maid. "You have let us see your mind at work; we know there is no evil in you. That your fortune should be our fortune is enough for me. You have said you will give the love of our men back to us, and though I don't understand how you will or can, I know you will."

One by one we swore loyalty to Vanue before all other greater beings.

Then Vanue looked at her Nor maids and said with a strange innuendo that made them laugh with delight and anticipation: "Now we must send them to school—in pairs!" The laughter of the gold-topped lilies of Nor rang merrily.

What sort of a school was this, I wondered, to make them laugh so?

The tubes took Vanue's train to the doors of her own cavern palace. Huge air locks swung open to admit the whole procession into the under parts of the palace. When we stepped out into the special air of her home that tremendous acceleration of the life processes that I had noted in her chambers in the space liner again seized us—and life became a thing to really fear to lose.

But as yet I had no inkling of what lay before me in the mystery of the wisdom that had built that place to house their first borne, Elder Princess Vanue, daughter of the Elder Gods of Nor.

Flinging off her wraps, which she had worn to the council chamber because of their significance, Vanue said: "We will put the children in school, and then to our own work. We have much to do to make ready and the time is short."

"School" turned out to be a vast laboratory—a replica on a much mightier scale of our own Titan technicon's laboratory school where Arl and I had learned to know each other and the possibilities of life. Instead of embryos, the nutrient tanks contained six foot ro and even much larger men and women.

Taking Arl and me in her hands she placed us in one of the big tanks. The liquids were warm and comforting and we splashed about playfully while others of our Atlan group were also being placed in pairs in tanks like our own.

Then Vanue's maids swarmed about us, placing wires about our arms, our wrists, our hands and feet; fastening breathing cups over our mouths; thrusting needles into our veins and attaching them to the ends of thin tubes; placing caps of metal with many wires connected to generators and other machines on our heads; covering our eyes with strangely wired plates of crystal.

I heard the tank cover sealed and more fluid gushed in until we were completely submerged. We floated in suspension within the tanks.

Then began a strange thing; for our minds, Arl's and mine, were conscious of each other through the medium of the interrelated wiring and the plates over our eyes—an awareness that must have been augmented a thousand times. Her breath was my breath, her thoughts took place in my head stronger than Vanue's ever had, and the woman-soul of her was so augmented in my mind as to eclipse all other woman's appeal that my memory had ever recorded.

A strange little voice (it must have been Vanue's speaking over a telethought instrument) whispered beside me: "You will never escape Arl now. You are her slave forever." And as I listened, I knew that Vanue spoke the truth.

Arl's face, laughing before me in the eye plates, became larger and larger, entered my brain, became the wellspring of my being. I heard Arl's thought, a vast river of force flowing in my mind, saying: "Where I go, there will you go also. The thing that is my desire is growing in you. My roots are your soul. You are my desire and the slave of my desire!"

And I heard my own thought make answer in Arl's mind: "So it shall be, always, oh maiden of the clicking hooves and swift hands, of the beautiful tail, of the clean will and strong desire!" And I knew that what I said was true.

The fluids and forces that were pulsing through us made these things grow within our beings, so that centuries of loving contact were replaced by minutes of furious growth; and we fell asleep, strangely within each other our thoughts, growing and becoming an integrant part of our being. Through every fibre of my body I could feel fecund growth swelling and expanding, patterned by thoughts which were mine and yet not mine. In my ears strange sounds beat mysterious meanings which were forces taking root within me. My memory was a vast garden of new thoughts growing as my mind grew, and remembering all the principles that came over the wires from the Elder Gods' own thought record.

Always overhead I could feel the Nor maids watching my mind pictures and correcting the growth memory so that everything took its rightful place. And within me I could hear Arl, sleeping and growing too, and she was very dear.

The thing that was me slept as a babe sleeps in the womb, and the seeds of the Gods' thoughts took root in Arl and me and grew. We were at once children asleep in the womb of the God mother, and man and wife wrapped in each other's adoring arms. Time flowed by like water; and we slept but were more awake and alive than ever before, and felt the pleasure of each the other's body and soul appeal, the very inner essence of man-life and woman-appeal to man. Life pulsed from each of us into the other constantly. We had more pleasure of each other in the growth school tank than ever I have known of in any pleasure.

Among the things that became a part of my knowledge was the promise of the future in such tanks as this: Sometime Arl and I were to build such a tank and appartatus and take a long sleep in it and awake as Gods, full of the strength and the beauty and the pleasure of life and life's fulfilment.

So it was that Arl and I were married by an actual mingling of the seeds of our being, and not by any foolish ceremony; blessed by the actual love of Vanue, now our Lady, and not by any meaningless words.

Though we were in the growth tank less than a week, we came out inches bigger in every way; but the real growth that had taken place was an inner growth—for I was vastly heavier and my strength was aware of new limits.

Mentally, too, I was vastly more able; for when I looked about at the apparatus I knew the inner construction and use of every bit of it, and I knew that from then on few things would mystify me other than the work of the very oldest Gods.

I found that I had not lost my love for Vanue, but that I loved her now as one loves and is grateful to a leader. My love for Arl was the strongest thing in me. [28]

All of us found out now that Vanue was not the most foolish of the Elders of Nor, despite her comparative youth, but was looked up to everywhere as one whose star was in the ascendant. Her followers were more numerous than many much more prominent Elders.

Arl and I spent several days together in our love, and in seeing the wonders of Nor's civilization. Here was a vast series of underground cities, all heated and bathed in beneficial energies artifically created. No need for a sun's light to live. No danger of dis-integratives from a dangerous sun poisoning the soil and water of the planet, to cause slow death by age.

Then one day Vanue called me to her.

"I speak now of the mission the Elders of the council granted to you in the conference chamber. As you remember, your part in the coming task is two-fold. In one phase of this you will accompany us to act with us in the great war that must be fought. We have developed a plan in which your help as an advance and secret agent is necessary. You will be told more about that later, when we have embarked.

"Now, however, your other mission begins, here on Nor. It is the mission of love for your fellow men. No matter how successful we are in rescuing the men of Atlan, it cannot be that we will rescue all of them. Many must not be rescued! There is nothing we could do for them, poisoned as they are to the point of death. Nor must we allow any of this poison to escape to the dark worlds where it can infect others. Too, the dero influence is dangerous, and madness must not spread over the universe.

"Thus it has been given to you to inscribe on imperishable plates of telonion, our eternal metal, a message to future man which will be placed on and in Mu so that those who have the intelligence to find and read it may benefit by the truths of growth and defense against a too-soon death by age.

"After the passing of Atlan science from Mu, men will begin to die at the same age, and their sons will all be the same size at the same age. This will be caused by accumulations of sun-poison in the water of Mu, which will stop all growth in mankind at almost the very beginning of their development. They will scarcely get beyond childhood before they will begin to die.

"These plates you will inscribe will contain a message that is a key and a path to the door that will open life value to these future men, whose fate we know and pity, but cannot prevent. We can only teach them what we know that will enable them to get the most out of their life on Mu. The dero will not be able to read, and thus will die as they should. Those whose minds are powerful enough to escape complete dero-robotism will read and profit.

"You can tell them how to attain this life growth by freeing their food and water intake of all the poisons that will be found in it in the natural state. The age poisons can be removed by centrifuge and by still; their air can be made a nutrient by proper treatment and freed of all its detrimental ions by field sweeps of electric. The exd on which the basic integration of life feeds can be concentrated (just as it was in your body in the growth school tank) in energy flows which greatly increase the rate of growth and the solidity and weight of the flesh.

"Tell future man to do these things, Mutan Mion, and their reward will be great. You have seen what the reward of such effort can be—in thousands of years of life's fullness—even on a planet under a detrimental sun. We cannot save those men yet unborn. We can only leave for them the heritage that is rightfully theirs, the heritage of our sciencon knowledge. And you, Mutan, in your infinite love and pity for your fellow men, shall perform this task with all the energy that your love makes possible!"

I left the presence of mighty Vanue, marveling at the understanding of the Elders and Gods of Nor. No wonder that their race is so great. To me, the humble artist of Sub Atlan, had been given a great mission; one that thrilled me to my depths. I hurried to Arl to tell her all about it.

"The wonder of it!" I exclaimed, having repeated what Vanue had told me, "In my hands—the simple-awkward, unskilled artist's hands of Mutan Mion, culture man of Mu—has been placed the hope of future man! To me is given the honor to preserve for men yet unborn the knowledge of their heritage of life!

Arl held me to her, and her eyes were shining. "Yes, I understand," she said.

"There is more!" I went on. "The Nortans set out soon to rescue many thousands of Atlans and Titans and their variform offspring from the threat of death by a dying sun's radioactives, and from the black death of the derodite; but I, Mutan Mion, am to be the rescuer of untold numbers of future men down through the history of Mu, until the very planet is dead! Think of it . . ."

Arl kissed me tenderly. "Go, Mutan, and busy yourself with the beginning of the message. You have but little time, and I think you should begin by putting down the story of Mu—our story!—and thus give body to the message to future man. Perhaps he will not even remember Atlantis! Nor Tean City, nor all the other vast cities of center Mu. Perhaps he will not even remember that there ever was such a being as an Atlan or a Titan or a Nortan. It will be your duty to tell him that, too, my loved one. For how can he believe and hope if he has no knowledge of the truth of life?"

"Most certainly must I tell them of you!" I exclaimed. "Never in all Time was there such a woman!"

And kissing her again, I hurried off to the sciencon laboratories to gather the materials necessary to begin scribing my imperishable plates of telonium with the message of hope to Lemurians unborn.

For many days I worked, putting down the truths and the knowledge to overcome the poison of age to the fullest possible extent, as it is now done in Tean City and all Mu; and the means to full life growth. I told the story of our flight from Mu, and much of the history of Mu. I told of the Titans and the Atlans who live throughout all dark space; who are seaching ever for new suns. I told of the Nortans; who do not believe in living near any sun, old or new.

I brought my message up to date—and barely in time. For when I had finished Arl came to me.

"Vanue's ship leaves for Mu in a few hours," she said. "You must be ready."

At that moment it hit me—these were my last hours with my loved Arl until I returned from the war in Mu; if ever I returned. Now for the first time since reaching Nor I knew sorrow. But Arl saw what was in my mind, and her words brought joy back to me.

"I am to go along, as operator of one of the telescreens on our own ship," she announced happily.

I should have known that my loyal Arl would never consent to remaining behind while I went into danger!

"Your life is my life," she was whispering as she snuggled in my arms. "Where you go, there also will I go. Your soul's nearness is my desire."

Footnotes

28 The "school" of growth to which Mutan Mion and Arl and their companions went for their growth in both body and mind is the concrete manifestation in apparatus of the science of mangrowth as conceived by the three ancient god-races. It was based on simple laws of the integration of matter. These simple laws are being set forth in a scientific monograph by Mr. Shaver and your editor, who firmly believe that its publication will throw a bombshell into all of present-day physics and chemistry. Naturally they cannot be dealt with in complete form here, but a slight explanation of what was done to Mutan Mion seems necessary. Part of this explanation is in the words of Mr. Shaver:

Growth is an inflow of exd. Life itself is a flame of integration, which like a fire must be fed or it goes out. Exd is the fuel of that flame, and by its condensation into matter, adds to the flame, causing growth. Naturally this growth is a material growth. What the Nortans did was to concentrate the flow of exd so as to feed the flame of life at a greater rate, and thus cause greater growth. A technical simile might be drawn: a fire, when supplied with finely divided carbon and a larger supply of oxygen becomes a greater, fiercer thing. It is the same with life. When supplied with a greater quantity of exd, it grows, becomes stronger, more active.

The mechanical means is very similar to the magnetic field lenses used in electron microscopes, which direct and focus a flow of particles called electrons into a beam more revealing than light because its particles are smaller. This same magnetic field principle can be used to focus exd and thus hasten integration. A magnetic field, lens-shaped, could focus falling exd by attunement just as a radio collects certain waves. This attunement can be determined by constructing a coil in the same shape as the coils of the electron microscope—but much larger. The focus can be determined by its light focus, which would be the same. A plant, placed beneath this point of focus, perks up its leaves, reaches out, is invigorated, exudes a dew, in a short time is twice the size it would ordinarily have been.

Once there was a book called the "T" book ('T' for integration, for growth force, energy, etc.) which was in rather widespread use up to the time of Christ. It contained the elemental frames of logic and simple what-to-dos like the age-poison elimination. beneficial generators, and so on. But some group feared its influence and it was destroyed, so completely that only the memory of that once infallible book remains, which memory was the father of the Bible and all its veneration, including the cross on its cover, the 'T' sign.

The direct need for a greater future for man is strengthening of the general mind by T forces, the growth of a better brain. No progress is truly progress unless man grows a better brain to grow a better brain. That is the pattern of progress—to grow a growth to grow, etc. What man needs is a conscious aim toward growth. To learn how to grow into a man better able to grow into a wiser man is a goal followed by but a few men out of all the number who could be striving in that direction. The great ones called such a goal 'TIC' and any energy not directed toward that goal was called 'ERR.' Alexis Carrel says much the same thing in 'Man, the Unknown.' He is one of the few men on earth whose efforts are not err to self interest. That is, he aims to understand his life process and make it last longer. True self interest is seen in his efforts, as in few others. These others think of self interest as an oppositional of other self interests—which is a de illusion (Atlan for disillusion), for oppositionals neutralize. True self interest would therefore always be a coincident, not an oppositional.

Our most basic concepts have become err from disintegrant force distortion of thought flows over the long period of time since we were children of the Gods of the past.—Ed.

CHAPTER VIII.

RETURN TO MU

It had been but a short month since our arrival on Nor. Many had been the preparations, most of them unknown to me. Only now as I went to the launching cradles did I see the full extent of those preparations. I found a fleet of mighty space vessels lifting from the frozen face of Nor, leaving to gather at a rendezvous in space.

Vanue's own vast vessel was not the least among the fleet, nor I and Arl the last aboard. On her viewscreens we watched countless other ships lifting on reverse gravity beams with what seemed to be almost utter ponderance until they reached a point in space where they could take up normal flight. New-built ships these were, wonderful in their engineering and armament.

We watched, also, many Nortans, mostly Nor war-maidens and Nor warro, embark on our own ship. Vanue herself was already aboard, together with several other Elders of minor stature. They brought with them vast quantities of material of unguessable use. Observing it I understood that their purpose was not wholly to save the people of my race from their sad plight, but to nip in the bud the growing power of Evil forces so near their own stead in space. That they were wholly confident of their ability to do this, I knew, but I knew also of the mighty armaments and endless warrens of the Atlan armies. I had seen their tremendous vessels maneuvering around Mu on the viewscreens and the news teles. I hoped the Nortans were not overconfident.

But as we proceeded into space toward Mu at greater speed. I found that I did not really know the Nortans. I had underestimated them. They understood concept, and I came to realize that concept had become a frozen thing on Mu by comparison. The Nortans used the truth, for it was the right conceptual attack. <u>Evil has no concept; it is a mad robot to detrimental force</u>. When Evil has power and men must obey or die, then only is it to be feared. But sometimes men fight for Evil unknowingly.

As we passed an Atlan space station a Nortan ship would land and presently take off again, followed by all the ships of the station. They had just told them the truth. The Nortans had an ancient reputation that forbade any doubt of their words. It was as simple, and as powerful, as that.

This went on so often, that as we neared Mu the Atlan fleet with us was nearly as large as our own. The truth can be a mighty friend and these space warriors knew the Nor-men and trusted them.

So impressed was I by the ships of this vast battle fleet that I was tempted to go to my quarters and describe them as part of my message to future man; but I abandoned the idea. I reasoned that if my message were a needful one when it was found, its finders would have little use for, or need of, such technical information as the construction of space weapons.

Perhaps when they learned again to fight the aging power of the sun and the evil her disintegrant force can bring to life, they could again learn such other things as they would need by searching space for friendly peoples. There was an idea—I would put down the information necessary to direct such a search. It would be a simple thing—for the great ones would never be found near or under the rays of a sun as old as this one will be by then. Aging suns would always be a space horror to be shunned by all men. Only the action of the derodite on Mu had kept our own Atlans so long under its rays. Only on or near dark worlds and new suns would the great ones be found.

It was while I stood at Arl's side watching still more Atlan ships join us that a thought came to me.

"How can the Nortans so quickly trust the ships of the Atlans as to allow a number of them near their own fleet?

"Silly," chided Arl, flirting her tail at my question, "they don't trust them. It is not a question of trust. They just place a very large female Elder aboard each ship as it joins our fleet and there is no further question of trust or obedience. Supposedly she goes aboard 'to advise the commander as to our plans and to interpret our ways to him,' but you know the real reason—"

"Of course!" I interrupted her with a rueful grin. "I should certainly understand from my own recent experience with Vanue!"

Atlan warriors are all male. Those commanders and their men would be unable to do anything else but obey, with complete loyalty. They could not do otherwise, for they could not find the will or wish to do it. Not even the commanders of space ships are Elders by any means. Under the spell of that vast woman-life, they would be helpless to her will in their ecstatic love for her.

There were maneuvers as we neared Mu, but I saw little of them. Most of the time I was busy with my telonion plates, inscribing further knowledge or duplicating them so that they might be deposited in Mu in many places.

Another job I had which took up much of my attention was the task of making thought-record from the heads of men in Atlan vessels nearby, in an attempt to learn what had happened in Mu since our flight. They knew little, for the telenews had evidently been as uncommunicative of Atlans' true troubles as before. Some whispers they had picked up, but nothing of great value.

I kept on, but it was of little use. They knew just enough to make them ready to join us, but no more. There was nothing that would help us in the coming battle. All we knew was that we were enroute to war upon an enemy who was undeniably powerful, but whose identity we would have no way of knowing—until he struck first! And that first blow might be a terrible one . . .

Noting some agitation in the ship I was watching, I focused on the commander's quarters just in time to hear the last of a general message from surface Atlan:

"—and since we hold the population under our war rays; and since the safety of that very population we know to be your objective; let me warn you that the very first sign of an attack on your part will be the signal for a general slaughter of the people on our part. They are only in our way anyway. You may kill us in time, but you will never attain your objective!"

The horrible import of the message stung me into inactivity for a moment, then I recovered and with haste swung my ray to hear Vanue's reaction to this problem-posing message. What would she reply? Or had she a reply to this development? Death for the very people we had come to save rested in her hands . . .

Then came Vanue's voice; and it held a world of bafflement in it, a note of defeat that opened my eyes wide in disbelief.

"Return to Nor," was what she said!

Return to Nor! Abandon our mission? No! It could not be. There must be a ruse in Vanue's mind. Vanue was not the kind to give up, even though the odds seemed great. Then what—

Vanue's voice in my mind said a single word: "Come."

I switched off my thought recorder ray and bounded down the corridor toward the great doors of hammered metal, a wild joy in my heart that at last she had need of me, and that certainly this was a ruse.

Even before I reached the great doors I knew one thing: Vanue's ship was not retreating toward Nor as the others seemed to be. Under cover of the swarm of retreating ships, our own vessel had slipped into the moon's shadow as we passed her and had come to a halt hanging there invisibly in the moon's earth lee.

Once I arrived before that vast flame of beauty I sank to my knees, but she reached out a great hand and raised me to my feet. From her desk she took a tiny box and showed me its one projection—a tiny stud; a switch.

"Take this and put it in your clothes. It looks like a pocket reading machine, and it will not be noticed with suspicion. In the locks an Atlan ship and pilot is waiting for you. He has been directed to take you to surface Atlan.

"Once there you will mask your thoughts in any way you please, for I know your ability in that respect. Then go to your old home in Sub Atlan. There turn on your telenews and wait beside it until you hear three clicks from it, repeated at uneven intervals. Then take out this box and press the metal stud full in. It will tell you what to do next. That is all."

I bowed low, kissed her foot's radiant flesh, and ran from her quarters.

The Atlan ship was waiting for me, the pilot ready and silent. He pointed out my old Atlan student's outfit, which was already aboard, and indicated that I was to wear it. I jettisoned my Nortan uniform and in a moment was once more Muton Mion, life-culture student of center Mu.

When I had completed my transformation I found that the ship was already rocketing down the regular passenger lane from moon to Mu. The pilot, an Atlan, spoke a few words of explanation and lapsed into silence.

"I am a taxi driver and you're a passenger. Mind that—and luck!"

It was all so simple. I could hardly believe it would work. But it did. The ship settled on the public field. I jostled my way into the tubes, and soon was roaring along toward my home—a student returning from an outing.

I switched on the seat telenews but apparently nothing was happening.

It recited the most inane occurences: a taxi motor failure had plunged two fares and the driver into the sea, and they had escaped with a ducking; a snakeman had caught his tail in a subway door, but would live; our adored chief Elder was having a birthday, may he have many more... I switched the telenews off. Anything could happen—and to Atlans nothing out of the way would even be whispered. Of the vast Nor fleet that had been so lately above, not the slightest hint. Great was the control of the derodite in Mu!

Not easy would be the task of the Nortan invaders!

Reaching Sub Atlan, I made my way to my own home, threw my hat at the old place on the hat rack, embraced my mother and kissed the tears from her dear face, slapped Foster Dad on the back and answered his grunted "Where in the whirling world of woolheads have you been wandering? with "Just sewing a wild oat. I'll tell you about it at dinner," and bounded up the stairs to my old room where I switched on the telenews and lay upon my bed, carefully masking my thoughts by thinking what tale I would make up to explain my outing to Dad.

Three sharp clicks from the telenews startled me. I had not expected the signal so soon. Vanue must have been watching. I leaped erect, drew the box from my pocket and pressed the switch. A voice came from the box.

"Put this box on your head and put your hat on tightly to keep the box in place. Do not take your hat off for any reason from then on. Go outside and walk around the block. Soon you will notice a strange thing; after which you will get more directions."

I did as directed, promising to return soon when I dashed past my astonished mother and father. I stopped only long enough to retrieve my hat.

Outside a strange drowsiness came over me. It was hard to move. The lights of Sub Atlan flooded the ways, but I ignored them and walked slowly around the block. I noticed the girl at the food tablet stand lolling fast asleep over her open cash drawer. How very careless of her, to sleep so. But then I found the service ro at the rollat stand also deep in slumber; and several of his customers sprawled in slumber on the seats with the doors open, the hood up.

The voice in my hat explained the mystery.

"By now everyone in Sub Atlan but yourself and certain others is asleep. So will you be if you remove your hat and the box, which gives off stimulating vibrants.

"Go at once to the administration center and switch off the auto watch and general attack alarms. Bind the chief Elder and anyone else who seems able to frustrate a landing. Then, wheneverything seems safe, put a communication beam on our position and guide us in"

The Administration building in Sub Atlan is a great tower which reaches not only to the roof of the cavern that houses Sub Atlan but through that roof and on up to surface Atlan, where it looms as the tallest building on the surface also. Great rollat ways connected the surface building with the sub building.

I activated a rollat at the curb stand, dialed the administration center's number, and drove the rollat by hand directly into the great hall and up to the doors of the council chamber. As I arrived I was surprised to see four of my comrades, Atlans from Vanue's ship, racing into the hall behind me from rollats at the curb.

I nudged the great doors with the rollat bumper. They held. Turning the thing I drove across the hall and came back at full speed, crashing into the great valves and at last they gave. I plunged into the hall, brakes squealing.

CHAPTER IX.

THE ABANDONDERO

Instead of finding the old chief Elder and his aides about the room, there was nothing. We raced through the place toward the telemechro center where the rodite mechs of the whole city were supervised by a concentration of screens which controlled them all when necessary. Upon these screens the whole city was watched, and could at any time be wholly robotized in an emergency from this point. [29] And here we found them, the controllers of the city; but they were not the giant elders I had expected to find. I broke into laughter at the sight of them.

Clothed in rags and dirt, hung all over with hand weapons, their hair long and matted, were the strangest, most disgusting creatures I had ever seen in my life. They were dwarfs, some of them white-haired, from the Gods know what hidden hole in Mu's endless warren of caverns.

"What in the name of mother Mu are these things?" I asked Halftan, who had been one of the Atlans arriving immediately behind me, and who now helped me in the task of binding the hideous dwarfs in turn after turn of the heavy drapes from the walls.

"You already know of them," he said. "They come from the abandoned caves and cities of Mu. When the machinery became defective from age, many centuries ago, a vast number of caverns were sealed up. Fugitives hid in them, used the defective pleasure stimulators, [30] and as a result, their children were these things.

"They die of age, are stupid, cannot even read or write, but they must have a vicious, cunning leader who has learned to use them. They are called 'abandondero' by the techs, who have captured some of them for study.

"If you had been in Tean City years ago, you would have heard them talked about on the telenews. The ones shown then were so stupid no one paid any attention. There is nothing so careless as a swelled head, I guess. Those supremely intelligent Elders of ours who should be tending this center will probably be found in ashes in the incinerator!"

His words wiped the laughter from my lips. No laughing matter now, these ugly dwarfs! They were dero, children of dero, enslaved in some manner by the derodite master who sought the death of all Mu! And the very fact of it brought home to me the greatness of the menace we were beginning to fight. For the first time I felt some misgiving as to the outcome.

We finished tying the filthy brutes and then turned our attention to the immense central synchronizing screen where a multiplex view of every station in the city could be seen. At each screen slumped the particular wizened dwarf who had been operating it, and who was now fast asleep and secured by our makeshift bonds on his limbs.

We activated the big space communicator, swung the beam toward the approximate position of Vanue's ship, sounded the 'ware' signal.

Instantly Vanue's face appeared on our screens—and we flashed the view beam on each of the bound dwarfs and on the big multiplex screen, showing the sleeping dwarfs who had replaced the original Atlan Elder's rodite. She nodded comprehension, not speaking. Then she switched off her communicator. We waited; it was up to her from now on. Meanwhile it was up to us to hold the fort here in the telemechro center.

"Thank Venus," said Halftan, his eyes aglitter with excitement, "these creatures are stupid, or we would not have overcome them so easily, nor would our job holding out here be as easy. Smarter operators would have managed to flash some signal when they sensed they were going to sleep."

I was inclined to agree that his analysis was correct. But I also added mentally that when no checking signals went out in the next few minutes, an investigation might be made from Tean City, or wherever the central control was located.

"Do you suppose our enemies never heard of a sleeper ray?" I asked Halftan.

"Did you, before you met Vanue and the Nortans?" countered Halftan. "Besides, these dwarfs are sub-dero, not thinkers! I remember from the old tech report on them in the news. I wondered then why no one made a move to clean them out, but concluded that it was because they could not think coherently enough to be a menace. I realize now, however, that our corrupt big-heads were using them even then by some means that they had discovered."

"I was not talking of these dwarfs," I said. "I am wondering about the rodite and the big-heads themselves."

Halftan's face grew thoughtful, and he began a watchful survey of the multiplex screens with a new tenseness evident in his body.

Both of us saw it coming at the same instant, and a shock of real surprise swept through us. The dark bulk of Vanue's great Nor ship showed on the screens shadowed over the great surface tower of the administration center. The lightless ship had drifted down the communicator beam! What power Vanue must have, not to need the lifter ray for landing! What unknown science to use a communicator beam as a pilot beam!

It hovered for a brief time, then the roar of its great jets became a maddening thing; and the ship lifted again into the night sky. Why had it come, and what had it done? Had it done anything?

Our wonder lasted only a brief time, for soon we saw Vanue coming into the center, dwarfing it, stooping low to clear the ceiling fittings. Swiftly after her came her Nor maids, a hundred or more of them; and a dizzying activity sprang into life about us.

A tender from the Nor ship was lying before the doors of the hall, and in and out we Atlans and Nor maids sped, trundling trucks of apparatus. Once emptied the tender returned to the surface. Under Vanue's eye the dwarfs were unbound and placed in their former positions, while a rodite beam was set up behind each screen. Now they were held in a ro beam from a Nor maid's mind, the slaves of her augmented will.

The hangings were replaced; the space communicator switched off; even the marks of binding were chafed from the dirt-encrusted wrists of the abandonero. Then we hid. To the view screens all was as before our entrance.

Vanue gave a signal, and somewhere in space the sleep ray switched off. The city came to life. That sleep had not lasted more than thirty minutes. Would the freaks from the lost cavern realize what had happened? On that question depended the lives of millions of people, all over Mu. Vanue had no doubt but that the derodite would carry out their murderous threat to kill the people if we attacked. Well, we had attacked, but in a way Vanue hoped would not be realized.

The telescreen from Tean City began sounding a constant call. The nearest dwarf, a hideous old woman, reached over and threw the circuit open. On the screen was the furious face of a fat Atlan. He was one whom I knew well from his appearance on telenews screens as a high official in construction.

"Where have you been?" he screamed at her. "Don't you know how tough a spot we're in? Your orders are to stay on duty until relieved."

The hag's hoarse voice answered, a groveling fear on her dirty old face.

"We had a li'l trouble. One stray Elder came in with a private key, nearly bumped us all before we did away with him. Everything is all right, else. Nothing to worry about. He didn't know what was doing—been away for a year. He's dead meat man now."

"Might have upset everything," the fat Atlan growled. But he seemed appeased by the news. "The overgrown fools. There aren't many of them left alive in Mu. Let me know at once if anything else turns up."

Behind him, on the rodite screen, before he turned off the beam, we could see a scene of mad revelry. In the background were the tremendous figures of some of the great ones of Atlan writhing in horrible torment while about their bodies crackled the blue flames of some paingening electric. Drunken renegades from Atlan's army reeled across the screen, dragging protesting girls after them. It was evident that they were celebrating the frustration of the Nor fleet in a manner deemed to be appropriate!

Then the Tean City screen went blank as the beam was switched off, and the old hag, her face a toothless grin at what she also had seen, reached out and broke the contact on the screen.

On the various units of the multiplex screen from the sub-rodite stations of surface Atlan and Sub Atlan cities much the same conversation took place. Each abandonero explained apologetically that he had fallen asleep and begged not to be reported. Each was reproved by the ro at the "plex" control.

We knew that they would never realize that all had fallen asleep. Many even denied their sleep, claiming they had had no signals. All reported everything all right.

"All right indeed!" I could hear mighty Vanue's thought in her furious mind. She waved her hand—and from somewhere in space that big sleep beam went on again.

On the multiplex screen at the center we could see Normen entering everywhere, setting up control apparatus without awakening the dwarfs. All over the sleeping city Nor-men were active, setting up hidden controls, ships landing and taking off—the armies of Nor gathering and entering the caverns . . .

Could they do it? Could they take the planet without setting off the alarm which would bring death down on the helpless people? As I looked at the sleeping, hideous things whose forebears had once been men, I felt they could. And when they did, I would not have wanted to be in the shoes of the Atlan or Titan who had trained and turned these things loose on the people of a whole planet! There would be a grim reckoning when the Nortans caught him.

"Vanue—Vanue!" called a Nor maid to her mistress.

"I have it! I have been reading the mind of this thing in its sleep. The center of this whole mess is not in Tean City nor any city, but in the abandoned caverns. Some ancient Elder, exiled long ago, returned secretly to Mu and entered those sealed cities. He has been chief of the abandonero for all their life. All their orders come from him. They do everything he says—nothing without his word. If we took the whole planet, we would still have his high and mighty madness to reckon with, together with a horde of these creatures who do his bidding—with Venus herself knows what kind of antique junk to do it. Some of those old war mech builders were not fools, and their methods were lost in wars when they were killed. You know, like the one time we ran into antique war mech on Helbal, when the deros of those old burrows used that stuff on us. No one knew what it was. We had to blow it all to Hades to get them."

Vanue picked her up with delight and kissed her. It was becoming increasingly plain to me that this was not the first time these warrior maids had seen action. They worked too smoothly. With the hand weapons and war weapon harness they wore, they were formidable looking Amazons. Their strength was unbelievable, and I knew it came from the inner growth of the incubator which increased the solidity of the flesh. My own period in the incubator had demonstrated that on my own body.

With the new knowledge the Nor maid had picked up, a new plan of action came into being. Vanue relinquished her authority in the telemechro center to one of the many space officers who had been going in and out on errands mysterious to me. Then the hundred Nor maids and ourselves accompanied Vanue to the tender and we were soon flashing skyward up the rollat tunnel and out into space.

Footnotes

29 The telemechro center was in itself under outside control, the communications mechanics being ro to the central control which was ro to the master control in its turn. Thus, all the rodite supervising the city could be placed under one master control through the screens in the telemechro center. By this means, the whole city's inhabitants could be placed under hypnotic condition, even including the rodite themselves. From this it can be seen the telemechro center is a vital spot in the dero control which had been thrown over all Mu.—Ed.

30 Entirely aside from our questioning of Mr. Shaver, we received a letter from him in which he describes the pleasure stimulator mentioned here. Or rather, he describes the sensations concurrent with its use in a very peculiar manner—since his words seem to indicate that he himself went through the experience. Whether or not the following words are those of Mr. Shaver, or of Mutan Mion, your editors have as yet been unable to determine. Certainly some of them are Mr. Shaver's (which only makes them more startling in their implications) and certainly some of them are not. In either case, they give us something to ponder upon.

"They played stim on me, a powerful augmentation of woman-love; to a hundred powers of natural love. There are no words to describe what this apparatus did for life. There were hundreds of rays about, always pleasant, their messages like conversation as though a thousand Scheherazades were telling tales at once. It augmented every cell impulse to a power untold. It seemed that every tree carried a beautiful face; every breeze was like a bath in elixir; every sensation having the value of a thousand nights of love. Little bells and visions of indescribable beauty mantled my closed lids to waft me into a sleep of dreams beyond anything mortal mind could devise." (Note the difference between the foregoing paragraph and the following.—Ed.)

"These mechs—rays—stim—have been used always as the forbidden fruit of life, the last treasure in the temple of secrecy which has consumed the ancient science. The orgies which the uses of such stimulants inspire have been going on secretly since the earliest times—beneath the temples and in the secret pleasure palaces of the world. (Shaver here seems to be talking of our modern world, not of ancient Mu.—Ed.) These orgies still go on, and are more deadly than before—more filled with de accumulated in the apparatus, the stim itself concealing the deadly rays whose effect is explained as the sad results of overindulgence; which is untrue—the stim is a beneficial of great virtue and leaves one stronger and wiser after use.

"The legend of the sirens is an example of ancient mechs which no one could resist—in the hands of evil degenerates it became a deadly attraction—drawing shiploads of men to death and the ships to looting.

"The course of history, the battles, the decisions of tyrants and kings—was almost invariably decided by interfering control from the caverns and their hidden apparatus. This interference, this use of the apparatus in a prankish, evil, destructive way, is the source of god worship, the thrill of divinity, the sensing of the invisible, the prostration of the will before the stronger will of the ray gen (ridden and unknown as it was)

"The remarkable part of it all is that it still goes on today. Emotional and mental stim—unsuspected by such as you and the average citizen—used in mad prankishness, all come from the ancient apparatus. If you will remember your stage fright in the school play, the many other times when your emotions seem to have gone awry without sufficient reason—were these natural?

"The dero of the caves are the greatest menace to our happiness and progress; the cause of many mad things that happen to us, even so far as murder. Many people know something of it, but they say they do not. They are lying. They fear to be called mad, or to be held up to ridicule. Examine your own memory carefully. You will find many evidences of outside stim, some good, some evil—but mostly evil."

Mr. Shaver gives this information in all seriousness. In the deserted (and not so completely sealed!) caverns of Mu, the dero descendants of the abandondero still exist, idiotically tampering with our lives by senseless use of the ancient stim mechanisms which actually were created to enhance man's life and not to plague it, but now are detrimental through an accumulation of radioactives which impair their action.—Ed.

CHAPTER X.

INTO THE TUNNELS OF THE DERO

Far out in Mu's nightshadow lay the silent fleet, dark and still as any lonesome rock drifting through space. We reached it and boarded Vanue's ship. Once aboard Vanue called a conference of fleet commanders, but we ro were excluded from it. Very obviously something very special was being planned that demanded no loopholes for a leak be left open. Not that we would consciously allow such a thing to escape our minds—but after all, we were only ro and far below the mental caliber of the Elders.

When Vanue came from the conference, her cheeks were flushed, she was beaming triumphantly, and her aura was pulsing madly. She went immediately into the tech laboratory of the ship and ordered two of the hideous abandondero brought in for examination.

They were placed in a telaug [31] and examined exhaustively for details of the lost caverns' entrances and exits and the location of the renegade Elder's power plants. Also we got a more or less clear history of what had been happening on Mu for many years; although the picture was about as clear as mud to the abandondero themselves. They had minds like rabbits—like mean rabbits now suddenly discouraged in their meanness.

For many years, most of their short lives, they had been stealing youths and maidens for torture and tormenting thousands of the Atlans with rays right in the streets.

ONE WORLD GOVN'MNT

When any Atlan had tried to do anything about it, it had only resulted in his death by one means or another.

How this idiotic dominance of theirs had been kept a secret for so long a time, while it grew stronger and stronger, was comprehensible only when we understood that the centralizing of all power by the rodite method of government had allowed complete control once the central rodite synchronizer was taken over. It had meant the sudden and complete end of Atlan government without even a suspicion that such a turnover had taken place.

When the center had gone bad no one had known. Even the abandondero couldn't tell us, except that they knew it had been long ago. Little by little, after the important coup, normal Atlans in charge of minor branches of the rodite government had been replaced by abandondero. The secret police had been killed off! By their strangle hold on the telenews centers all knowledge of such deaths and disappearances was kept from the Atlans. By continually checking over people's minds for any who were becoming suspicious, any trouble could be checked before it started.

For Venus knows how long they had been picking off the best brains of Atlan, the very flower of our race; doing them to death day by day, and no one was ever the wiser.

Much of all this we had to guess, for the abandondero actually knew little of the master organization beyond their own vicious experiences; but they knew their ancient warrens well and we could deduce approximately, from the ugly, half-formed images in their minds, where our objectives lay.

With this information in our possession, we went into action. In a very short time a host of tiny winged planes were dropping silently toward the vast culture forests where the hidden degenerates had made tunnels to the surface to gather fruit.

These planes were sealed-cabin helicopters, equipped for short flights in space by auxiliary gas jets, silent and flareless.

Our primary objectives were certain tunnels which held cables running to Tean City as well as other tunnels which held cables connecting the depths with the surface.

I kissed Arl lingeringly before I stepped into one of the planes and took off for Mu's forest-covered surface and became just one of many dropping motes that looked harmless enough but which carried more might than had ever before been gathered into such compactness.

We landed and made our way into the tunnel nearby. It led down steeply, and was a very ancient thing once we had gotten beyond the area constructed by the dero. It led soon into vast caverns housing long-abandoned cities.

These ancient ruins in the lost caverns were impressively eerie things. They had been built, I knew, in the early days of Mu, when under the new sun all growth had been furious and undying, with a fecundity scarcely to be imagined in present-day Mu. Most of the people who had once lived here had long ago become too big to stay in Mu; had gone to larger planets under other suns, or to huge, cold, planet-cities that drift in dark space. From what they had left behind I became more and more convinced that Mu's youth was too much in the past to have any more future. The planet should have been abandoned long ago. Just the contemplation of these mighty, long-gone glories in comparison with the lesser marvels of the best of modern Tean City was enough to tell the story to even the most thoughtless of Atlans.

Our lights played over the deserted, awful, death-like glory of the ancient mansions and even the hue of them gave off melancholy. However, to the warro and war maids accompanying me, such thoughts as those were not in order. Instead they kept sharp eyes and minds open for danger. What weapons lay unused in these tremendous fortresses from Mu's wild youth only the oldest of Elders could guess. And which of them might suddenly prove to be manned by warriors of the renegade Elder was something we could not know. But from the portent of their presence we realized that our enemy might be a tougher nut to crack than we dreamed.

As we marched down the silent, dust-laden ways, sleep rays and augmentative detectors of several kinds played miles ahead of us. Now and then we came upon a modern rollat, wrecked against the wall of a building, a dero asleep in its seat. They had crashed because the auto drive would not work here—check rays at corners and building entrances not being activated.

It was not many hours before our communications beams told us that the enemy cables had been cut; and so far as could be determined all dero communication beams had been tapped with false answer equipment and ro placed in attendance. So far our march into the depths had been accompanied by signal success. Next would come the actual locating of and the attempt to reduce the cavern stronghold of the renegade dero Elder. Rolling behind us as we advanced came an endless line of burden rollats, bearing war rays whose potency was incomprehensible to me. But I could guess from their complex construction that here were things that could loose terror itself. Before many hours I expected to see them go into action, loosing terror upon the author of the fear that had ridden hag-like upon the back of Tean City and all Mu's Atlans for many years.

It was then that I got a shock—for a big carry-all came riding by and in it, among the warrior maids bearing the crest of Vanue, was Arl... lovely, smiling, brave Arl of the cloven hoofs and defiantly flirting tail!

She flashed her teeth at me gaily as though she were on a picnic!

What is there about danger that accentuates the man-life in a man? As that smile played on me, the whole cosmos whirled in my head. I felt even more powerfully than I had in the duo-incubator the sensations of one-ness that existed between us. Comets buzzed in my head and I felt the urge for battle surge up in me; battle to preserve for myself and all others happiness such as was Arl's and mine.

Then, as we skirted a vast city bowl lit vaguely by a kind of marsh light that glimmers in these old warrens, action came! A dis ray raved out at us suddenly from a dark pile in the bowl several miles away. It cut great gashes in our columns before the swift, silent answer from the ray rollats had reduced the whole pile to silence.

Gray dust rose in a cloud over the bowl city as we swarmed into that huge old city-center building; and the horror that we found inside cured me forever of all sun lit planets. These devilish abandondero had a meat market in the lower floors, filled with human flesh; and a pile of choice cuts I saw was composed mainly of Atlan girl breasts! These dero things were cannibals and lived off immortal Atlan flesh!

So much for our illusion of benevolent government! How long had it been composed of hidden, grimming cannibals, the whole of our race unaware of its ultimate fate? I realized now that it takes more than patriotism and fine words over a telescreen from a ro face to make a state a safe place in which to live.

Because of a degenerating sun, all our apparent tremendous scientific advance had been set at naught by a few madmen... with these dero creatures eager to do anything the madmen said in return for a little fresh human meat. I saw now the fatal weakness in centralized government. One silent grab at that neck of power lines had resulted in death for the whole cream of the race. The awful power in telaug rodite methods of rule had only served to place the total wealth of the planet in mad criminal hands.

Yes, Halftan is right! There is "no thing so careless as a swelled head." To see sweet Atlan girl breasts displayed as a butcher's merchandise set a fury to raging within me that will not cease so long as de makes dero!

Thousands of the ragged, filthy abandondero lay about the huge building, unconscious from our rays, and we put them rapidly under telaugs to get a complete picture of their strength and the location of their other forces. Once we had gained our information they did not live long! We could not think of them as human things, these slaves to the disintegrant impulse to destroy that courses through all matter under an aging sun; and perhaps we, too, in this moment of horror, felt within us the effects of the sun poisons.

The children of the abandondero lay about naked or with a few rags draped on them, usually with a human bone they had been gnawing upon or playing with clutched in their hands. Vanue had all of the children gathered up and sent back to the ship "to treat them and use them to people a small planet as an experiment."

"Let that planet be far away!" was my thought.

We had learned from our searching of the minds of the abandondero that the old Exile's stronghold lay far in, nearly at center Mu. Yes, the rot had progressed far in Mother Mu. Always in my mind the most amazing fact of this rot will be the extent of its influence on the pattern of Mu's life-supporting energy flows. This dictating pattern had been so effective that their plight was not known nor hardly whispered of by any of the Atlans. Yet they were slaughtered indiscriminately, sold as meat to the abandondero, and the gods know what else they had put up with for how many years with the sickening realization that to appeal to higher-ups for help would spell death. All these years . . . without managing to make their plight public knowledge!

The telaug records told us that many of the dero had been torturing and tormenting Atlans all their life, and eating them too. Yet the news systems had managed to ignore all such tales, partly from individual fear of consequences, and partly from a dread of being considered mad for harboring such suspicions. There is no cloak for corruption like the average citizen's supreme faith that all is well as long as the paper is delivered, the telenews functions without saying anything alarming, and the dignitaries strut their pompous fronts regularly as upholders of righteousness.

I could see what had made them so supremely blind now. It was the effects from which the migration had been intended to save them. Yes, that migration had been delayed too long by a few centuries, it appeared.

It was another thing for me to stress in my message to future man; to inscribe on my timeless plates of telonion. Those who will people this planet again with children from the seed of the few we will not be able to find and rescue must be warned that there can be no peace nor beauty in life under this sun, except that they build special chambers which exclude detrimental forces as well as the radioactives that cause age.

Just so long as Mother Mu spins under this sun, just so long will her energy fields induct disintegrant charges from her destructive force, and these charges will work out into neutralization of man-matter growth through destructive will in the units of the life pattern. Without extraordinary precautions these detrimental forces will result in continual war and complete stalling of all real racial, social and individual growth.

If one of future man's really healthy men creates a machine of value to his people, one of the destructive men will take the same machine and destroy that same gain with it. l3isintegrant energy must be neutralized by an equal amount of healthy integrant energy. If it is not, this disintegrant energy will work out in continual social troubles, famines, diseases and death—if it does not actually take the form of a war.

This need not be the fate of future man! The life which grows in integrative source material concentrating chambers can be safe, immortal life—but all life outside such chambers will be destructive, if not by actual fierce blows, then by stupid interference and destructive disapproval.

These are the truths I, Mutan Mion, culture-man of Mu, realizing even more forcibly now, must pass on to future man, written on tablets that will be deposited in likely places so that they may be found in some future time. These truths—in addition to a history of the great war I am now observing; a war which wishes to save all future men, but which cannot, because of those lost ones of the forest whom we will never be able to search out—must reach future man! [32]

Footnotes

31   Telaug—a machine which augmented and strengthened telepathic signals so that even the most secret thoughts could be read.—Ed.

32   Judging from the information recorded by Plato, as received from Solon, it would seem that these metal plates so often mentioned by Mutan Mion (which this manuscript definitely states were deposited in many places both inside and upon the surface of this planet) were deposited about 12,000 years ago. Since such vast upheavals of nature as the sinking of Atlantis, the smashing down of the gates of the Pillars of Hercules and thus forming the Mediterranean Sea, have occurred, it would seem that the hiding places of these plates more than likely have been destroyed and rendered impossible of discovery. At least, science has no record of any such plates having been unearthed; nor is there any such record in legend or history beyond the possibility of the plates of the Ten Commandments given (found?) by Moses upon the mount. However this seems unlikely, since they are described as being of stone, which seems true since they were smashed by Moses in his anger. Apparently the message over which Mutan Mion labored so mightily has never been found.—Ed.

CHAPTER XI.

BATTLE TO THE DEATH

At distances of a hundred miles and more the battle was joined at last. We surrounded the old fire-head, [33] ex-Elder Zeit, of Atlan in his center-Mu lair and succeeded in cutting him off without alarming Tean City or any other post so far as we could judge. We knew the dero would not use the destructive machines to kill the people without word from the old master of murder. And they would not get that word; for our ro sat astride all communications.

But the old idiot himself was actively alarmed! Every weapon that ones-time Atlan stronghold held was throwing fire and death through every boring we could approach him by. Nor-men died by the thousands (and they are not enamored of death for they have much to live for!) before we finally brought up enough shorter [34] ray to ground those tremendous flows of hell-fire from the ancient generators. Zeit's hideout was a super arsenal!

Now our own needle rays concentrated on a single spot in the old fortress' metal walls. That metal, we knew, had been hardened in the past by subjecting it to exd flows of great strength. [35] It would resist most rays, but it was just a matter of throwing enough dis at a small enough opening point till the metal began to blaze and flow in a stream.

The opening grew larger, but the defenses of old Zeit were a long way from being pierced. Our own forces were protected both by conductive fans of rays which grounded any ray that threatened us and by flows of energy which were so strong that any ray that struck them was repelled or swept out of existence by the out-massing kinetic of the cone of force. But since these rays coned out at Elder Zeit's dero fortress on a level with its walls, there-was little overhead to protect us. It was an opening for Zeit and he took advantage of it!

From the towers of black metal suddenly sprang whirling comets; electrical vortices packed with howling energy in circular motion, which can be thrown in such a way that their circular motion causes them to describe an arc, for the same reason that a pitched ball curves. These arcing electronic cannonballs curved over our outflung protective wall and, striking our lines, bounced and leaped unpredictably from one point to another, searing everything within a dozen feet of their erratic path.

A few of these would not have mattered, since their behavior was uncontrollable, but they came flaming over by the thousands and set the whole army into confusion, dodging about, trying to guess where the howling, whirling, pausing, leaping things would go next.

Since many of our men had to leave their controls to dodge the rolling fire, their retreat almost became a rout when old Zeit threw a hellishly dense concentration of dis on our protective fields, breaking it down before our remaining men could swing enough counter-force into action to neutralize it, burning down our grounding conductive rays; and boring a huge hole through our center.

As I watched in horror, my mind was unable to gasp this paradoxical truth. How is it that mere mechanisms can so rout intelligent men? The same intelligence built these machines, long ago. Now, seemingly, it confounds that intelligence, seeks to and almost succeeds in destroying its creator.

But our Nor giants had a few tricks left up their sleeves. I suspected that they had not been used because it had been unthinkable that the old devil of a dero Elder could have outreached us. Conductor rays soon dissipated the charges in the fireballs; an out-massing bank of force ray generators replaced the burned-out breach in our protective fields.

Now our men had time to carefully fine down the focus of our needle rays to a more and more concentrated beam of dis force. Then simultaneously placing all the needles on a predetermined point, usually at the base of the openings where Zeit's deros worked at their ray guns, they beat down the flashing black sweep of Zeit's counter-conductive concentration, . . and his deros died at their controls.

This went on for hours as the dero were replaced by others under the devilish Elder's will—only to be killed again by the dancing, unpredictable needles of death which went through anything when they suddenly all swung to one point.

All the time cutter needles gnawed steadily at the rock roof of the great bowl, directly over the ancient black-walled fortress. Chunks of the superhardened rock rained down. It was tough stuff; tougher than steel. As soon as the artificially hardened surface of the rock was cut away the soft body of the rock above could be cut down in masses huge enough to cover the renegade Elder's hideout completely.

The walls and roof of the metal fort gave out great brazen clangings as the rocks fell from the height.

Still the fiery vortex spheres kept pouring from the black towers in steady streams, only to be caught by repeller beams and flung aside.

Force needles cut doggedly at the tower's sides and one by one they toppled with a great thunder of metal on metal and a fury of blazing-arc force from torn power cables.

Over the whole blazed a fiercely dancing flare of blue and purple flames from the clash of dis rays with the neutralizing fields. It was more and more evident that the end was approaching for the abandondero's feared master! A great exultance was growing in my heart as I foresaw the end which must soon come.

To corroborate my vision of nearing victory, interceptor ro of the falser-answer communicators sent us a message that Zeit was calling wildly for help.

"Nothing is so pleasant," went the report, "as to sorrowfully tell him that we're unavoidably detained by pressing engagements."

But in my mind now came a darker, sobering thought.

It was the thought wave of Vanue, impinging on my brain. "What will his last effort be?" I heard her muse.

I had caught and repelled a couple of vortice balls on my beam that might have approached her and had been dreaming of what form her reward might take—but now that thought left my mind. If Vanue had reason to worry of what Zeit might have up his sleeve as a last desperate gamble, I too had reason to be concerned.

I watched the battle with more sober contemplation, peering ever for signs of some final development that might be dangerous.

Then as I watched for it came the thing that is always feared in battle; the unseen factor that suddenly upsets all calculation. From somewhere the dero had unearthed a tremendous levitator. [36] We ourselves had a few with us to get the heavy stuff over tough going; but this one was a monster, once used in construction. This thing began lifting the masses of rock that had fallen on the fort, lifting them and dropping them from high in the air upon our lines.

Our own lifters were not big enough to handle the tremendous masses that kept dropping on our ranks and smashing the protective force-beam generators. When several of the generators had been crushed, the old devil used the master beam of the old fortress and bored through the openings, burning a path of destruction. Our whole enterprise was endangered—even faced total defeat!

I could hear Vanue's mind racing madly, "What to do? What to do?" And because of her confusion and anxiety, I knew how desperate our situation was indeed. Never had so great a fear filled my heart as I watched with staring eyes the havoc old Zeit was causing in our lines with his great super-ray.

As fast as our needle rays found the thing, new dero rushed in, moved it, went on with its deadly work. However, a concentration of conductor rays finally bored through to its base, shorted its vast power down to our size. Now we could handle it!

But our losses had mounted horribly. As I gazed upon the slaughter, I could not help but think that with our superior mental equipment all this should have been avoided. I am afraid there was criticism of our Nortan minds in my thoughts at this moment...

Vanue's thought came into strong being in my head, answering my unspoken denunciation.

"Detrimental force has an automatic electric play about it that strangely serves for thought. It is hard, no, impossible, to predict; as our healthy minds neutralize detrimental force, cannot therefore 'think' it. Too, in these conditions, their telaugs read our minds and our own imagination works against us. Healthy men are naturally too optimistic to foresee trouble fully. Then, beside that, no one knew or could know that the old fortress in here was so heavily equipped. Old Zeit nor any of his retainers have been out of the place for nearly a century. He kept the mech secret with very rigid care. People have gone into his fortress, but none have come out. The tunnels that lead down to this place are all too small to bring real war equipment down from the surface. We are really near the center of Mu. And on top of that, we have been a little over-confident, due to the unintelligent appearance of the dero. Who would expect such things to put up a fight?"

Her voice ceased in my mind, and I no longer fostered the thought that all this death could have been prevented. I felt a deep shame for even harboring the thought, and a deep gratitude for the favor she had bestowed on me in explaining so patiently even while she was in the midst of the greatest battle of her whole career. Such honor had never before been bestowed on a simple ro, I was sure.

Now, as I returned to my contemplation of the battle, I saw that our sleeper beams were following our dis rays' openings in Zeit's force shields, but they seemed not to have the desired effect. The old ogre must have had some means to jerk his harried dero awake as fast as they dropped off. Possibly some type of stimulator ray—a clever use for stim, I thought; ordinarily they are for entertainment.

Finally, however, we swept the whole place with a concentration of dis rays and sleeper beams and the boulder-covered pile of horrors fell silent. A few beams still played from the heap, but they were evidently automatic watch beams with no one awake behind them.

Our own lifters now cleared a path for our rollats to the doors. At last it was time to enter and mop up. As we went forward, I heard Vanue's ever-cautious mind warning me to "Watch out for the devil's joker" as our rollat-mounted rays moved up to the wall's lee and started blasting away at the doors. We rolled over the blazing mass of their remains and were inside. Atlan's leech had been loosened!

The place was three-deep in corpses. Many of them had been Atlan warriors; whether captives driven by Zeit's or his rodite's will or renegades I could not say. They lay at the white-hot projectors, their hands burned free of flesh, the bones still clasping the red-hot controls. Powerful indeed had been Zeit's ro compulsion.

We found the vast mountain of flesh that was ex-Elder Zeit of old Atlan. He was snoring among a mass of synchronizing rodite apparatus as big as a city block. It was both antique and modern in construction, much of it evidently salvaged from ancient ruins. Zeit was a three-hundred-footer, and he was not only big, but amazingly fat from his soft life in his hideout.

It was going to be a real job to get him to the surface alive. It would not be surprising if the soldiers found it necessary to take him apart and reassemble him later on.

The realization that we were going to move him to the surface was a surprise to me, because not to blast him into nothingness the instant we found him had seemed to me to be infinitely more than godlike emotional control in itself. But that the huge and evil head might contain technical secrets of value I realized when I thought of it.

We bound him with endless turns of steel cable, lifted him with a dozen of our levitators, and started him floating along toward the surface. Before he arrived, I'll wager he scraped a few turns in a rather painful manner, and not by accident either!

Other things we found in old Zeit's fortress—things that horrified us. He had had a couple of dozen Elder captives. It is one thing to see a broken man of my size, but to see the living remains of a Goddess Elder broken by torture until she had become a whimpering, cringing, babbling thing to pity did not quiet the rage in my breast, rage that I could see and feel burning in the Nor-men around me.

There were many captives still living, of all sizes, many women and girls—but most of them were in horrible shape from their treatment, and the others nearly insane from waiting for the same torture. I saw the endless variations on the torture theme old Zeit had devised to amuse himself in the centuries he had spent hiding in this place—as we recorded it on the thought record from his ro's minds.

I was placed as a guard over some of the antique equipment reserved by Vanue for her research. As I stood there, I could read the thoughts of many of the Elders who passed by after having viewed the gibbering things Zeit had made of Atlan men, women and Elders. I knew that if what they were thinking ever came to pass, Zeit would receive the equivalent of his tortures in Nor before he died—if he were allowd to die!

Now that the battle was over, more important Nor Elders arrived. Vanue's father was among them, and I heard him speak to a comrade. Vanue stood beside him as he spoke, listening as I did.

"I see that exile for him was a large Atlan mistake. To humble the exalted and to release them to work out their revenge at leisure is to create a devil and give him leave to harm you. These Elders he has been so lavishly entertaining in so terrible a way are the very ones who sat at the council which expelled him. Obviously they were a bit too gentle with a monster who sold his own people as slaves and got caught at it."

Vanue turned briefly to me, and once again I discovered how close she kept track of me.

"Zeit's joker never materialized, Mutan... and your reward for diverting the vortice balls will not be forgotten. It is a good religion, the word 'reward'. [37] Do not forget it."

There is a peace about being read by an understanding mind. Vanue would always know my intent toward her. I was her ro, until someday I would graduate into true self-determination. It was enough.

"Tean City still to take," I was thinking aloud a few minutes later, and suddenly realized that Arl, somewhere in the fortress, operating her telescreen beam, had been secretly watching me—for her voice sounded in my ear in answer.

"They got wind of what happened some way. Missing messengers, false reports exposed, or something. Anyway, they loaded up some of the finished migration ships, destroyed the rest, and took off. But I would say the abandondero migration has been too long delayed just as was the Atlans'—the Nor fleet will hunt them down like rats."

Hovering in the air before me her face appeared, materialized by tele-projection, and she bent forward and gave me a kiss with full augmentation. I reeled from the vital charge and nearly fell, but wound up on my knees asking for more. She went on speaking as if the tremendous kiss she had given were a nothing.

"They just made it, too. They tried to wipe out the Tean City population, but our men were entering from the lifts and from the tubes and laid down a blanket of conductive till none of the police corrective ray about the city would function at all. With the exception of the rockets on the ships, none of their mech would work.

"I think the Nor-men let them operate the lifter beams and the rockets to get them out into space where they can't hurt anyone."

And now Arl gave me the encore I had been begging for—but while she had been talking she had coupled on a booster circuit and the resulting kiss stretched me flat on the ground with a bump on my head as big as a dodo's egg.

I got to my feet to find her image gone, and the faint echo of her laugh still in my ears.

A few days later and Mu had been cleaned up. The victorious Nortan armies set up a temporary council of surviving Elders, who were few enough, to act in place of the real government that had not existed on Mu for nearly a century because of the coup of old Zeit. This council decided to take Nor advice and start building a home in a cold planet, far from any sun's evil influence.

A planet with untouched coal deposits located near the Nortan group of planets was chosen as the Atlans of Mu's new home. Work ro were dispatched to commence borings into the planet and to begin building the huge, steam heated, ray-drenched greenhouses in which Normen live and know so well how to build.

In a few short months the first ships took off for New Mu, and the last of the race of Atlan soon followed, abandoning Mu for their new home in space. Arl and I remained on Mu to the last. During this time I finished my telonion message plates and distributed them in the most likely places both in and on the surface of Mu. I pray that the descendants of those few wild men I have seen in the culture forests but have been unable to approach, may someday find these plates and have the sense to read them and heed their message. Someday, I have a feeling, they will be a race of men again. It is good seed they inherit, and they might be worth my effort in spite of the sun.

I pray that when they find the plates they will understand!

THE END

Footnotes

33 The word "fire-head" used here does not mean that Zeit was a hothead, or impetuous, or any other similar modern meaning of the word. It has a deeper significance, denoting his mental condition. For a complete definition the reader is referred to footnote 17. Old Zeit's head, his brain, was infected by the ever-fire of the sun, and the infection was so derogatory to this thinking processes that the only possible result was detrimental thought culminating in murder, the most detrimental of all thoughts. The reader is here requested to note the word "derogatory," an accepted word of our English language, which has as its root the ancient Lemurian word "dero." Note that the ancient meaning has come down unchanged!—Ed.

34 By the word "shorter" Mutan Mion does not mean the rays brought up were not as long, but that they were capable of "shorting" the energy flows from Zeit's generators. They must have been ionizing rays which served in much the same capacity as lightning rods, grounding the destructive beams hurled at the Nor-men before they were able to strike their target.—Ed.

35 This principle of "hardening" metal and stone so that they become unbreakable (used to prevent the roofs of the cavern cities from collapsing) has been mentioned several times in this manuscript. It is accomplished by forcing additional exd (which the reader will remember is the ash of disintegrated matter, or more properly, the basic energy from which matter is again integrated) into the substance to be toughened until it reaches a state whose ultimate end would be what we today conceive of as neutronium. By adding more matter, packing it so to speak, into the interstices between the particles of matter, a greater density and therefore a greater cohesiveness is obtained. This cohesiveness is actually the "in-flow" of gravity.—Ed.

36 A levitator is a portable lifter beam generator. Some of them are very small, and can be carried in the palm of the hand, or in the pocket. They were in common use for all tasks in Mu, and from Mr. Shaver comes the amazing statement that some of these portable levitators have been found in modern times and their secret use has given rise to the belief in the ability of "mediums" to use levitation of objects as one of their tricks in their seances. Perhaps most noted of these mediums was Mr. Daniel Dunglas Home, wizard, whose seances were the sensation of the United States and of Europe, the incredible recount of which was recently presented in "Magazine Digest." His feats of

levitation are indisputable, being vouched for by such persons as Princess Pauline Metternich; Austrian Ambassador, Prince Joachim Murat; Mme. Jauvin d'Attainville. Home was born in Currie. near Edinburgh, on March 20, 1833. Among his abilities was the power to see events happening a great distance away; the ability to "elongate" his body as much as a foot; and at one time he caused Ward Cheney, silk-manufacturing titan, to be lifted three times into the air while he "palpitated from head to foot with contending emotions of fear and joy that choked his utterances." (The reader should note the amazing similarity to many of the mechanisms of ancient Mu—the emotional stim; the levitator; the tele.) It was after he became the darling of such figures as Napoleon III, Eugenie of France, Alexander II of Russia, and Elizabeth Barrett Browning that he developed his "body elongation" trick and a still more sensational one wherein he placed his face among burning coals, bathing it as in water; without any sign of a burn. Is it possible that Home "discovered" his abilities in an ancient cave?—Ed.

37 This reference to the word "reward" as a religion is mystifying. and Mr. Shaver has never explained it. However, our thought on it is what might be termed the basis for all religions—the incentive to do good because of the hope of a reward of some kind. This seems the correct view when we consider Vanue's insistence that a service of good is never left unrewarded. It is logical to believe that loyalty would remain constant so long as the reward always certainly comes as a consequence of each demonstration of that loyalty. If nothing else, Vanue was an excellent psychologist, and a brilliant leader. Also she protected, as well as rewarded, as her reference to the "joker" demonstrates.—Ed.

THE RETURN OF SATHANAS

A Novel of the Revolt of
Evil Against the Gods.

—By Richard S. Shaver

CHAPTER I.

QUEST OF THE DARKOME

"Satan, with vast and hauty strides advanced,
Came towering, armed in adamant and gold."

—John Milton

The pursuit needle indicated a dizzy succession of zigs and zags in front of my straining eyes. The huge dread-nor, the Darkome, slewed in sickening curves as my hand on the swivel-jet stick tried to follow the crazily dancing needle. Was it—or was it not—the erratic ion trail of a dodging ship?

"Are we following one ship or a dozen?" asked Lt. Tyron, tightening the straining straps of the co-pilot's chair beside me.

"I don't know—but sure as the God's vengeance we're following something with plenty of reason to want to escape. And we will follow as long as the fool's drivers leave us a trail.

"Too much trail right now. A few more of those sudden jerks and either the Darkome or me is going off in two directions at once—and the Darkome is tough."

"There's no question we can catch the ship or ships on this trail, but, what I am wondering ... what has me worried ... is, will our quarry be a big enough fish to be important, or some expandable decoy of Sathanas?"

I turned from my inspection of the dials and looked at my first officer. Tyron was a good man, but too impatient for action and too continually worried that he wouldn't see any. But he was intelligent and, in the two centuries he'd been in my command, there had never been a question of his reliability. He had the familiar look of fearing that action was going to get away from him again. I couldn't help laughing down at him.

"Well, Tyron, before this is over you'll have a chance to catch a lot of those devils—and when we do you may get those hands you're so proud of, singed. Carry on!"

I settled myself in my seat before the universal view screen [1], thinking, "There's nothing to do now until we catch sight of whatever is making this trail." I, myself, was as impatient for action as Tyron, but in the long years since I left the culture farms of Mother Mu, I had learned to restrain my desire for adventure until the opportunity came to unleash my energies into effective action.

The irritation I felt at being forced to stay on duty was just another score I had to settle with the fugitive fleeing through space somewhere ahead of us. Here, aboard ship, I have my duty, and when it is performed, the course checked and affirmed, the log set to rights, and my officers assigned to their special duties, my time is my own. And woe betide the unfortunate who unnecessarily disturbs my meditations and experiments in my own ship-board laboratory. It is a well equipped laboratory—befitting the ennobled station the Gods of Nor have seen fit to bestow upon their humble servant and brother. Only in the capital cities of the God race are there comparable laboratories. I have spent years and many a long voyage in some of the less frequented reaches of space to equip it for the work I do when I am not on the errands of the Gods. Full of apparatus picked up in the strange ports of a thousand far off planets—perhaps a little evil-smelling at times, but it is my life, and in it is life—little lives whose efforts are at times vastly more successful than man's own . . . poor doomed mankind whose glorious ancestors are the immortal gods themselves.

On most of the assignments that I took my ship, the Darkome, I had plenty of time for my own experiments, far from the distracting social activities of my own adorable Arl. But this trip would not allow me any time to myself—this trip was ordered by the great Elders of Nor themselves. I was to capture and bring to trial that unwise but accomplished fiend, Sathanas, Ruler of the planet Satana. Sathanas, though a younger member of the God Race, had started his own private revolt against all authority—and the dicta of the Elders are not so lightly flaunted by any upstarts a few score centuries old. He had violated the Elder laws designed to protect and foster life and growth—it seemed that he could not get enough victims for his orgies of cruelty under the existing laws and had set out to make a few laws of his own. But, as I said, the laws laid down by the myriad Lords of Nor in Council are not easily broken—even by a powerful and cunning master of sin like this Sathanas—and thus it was that I sat on the bridge of the war vessel, Darkome—the crew alerted for battle action—its glistening hull plunging toward the general area of the planetary system that gave me birth long years ago.

Once his defection [2] had been fully exposed, Sathanas escaped our avenging fleet by the barest seconds. The ships in his fleet—several hundreds in numbers—had blasted up in the very face of our fleet—jockeyed into position in the center of the 'zone of weightlessness' [3] between the planet Satana and her satellite Feon—then disappeared in that fierce burst of full acceleration into light speeds that is only possible in the precise center of such zones of weightlessness. To make the maneuver more untraceable, every ship in the enemy fleet disappeared in a different direction. Perhaps we could have followed a few of them, but never would we find all of those divergent trails at many light speeds into the depths of space.

Of course, they must have had some pre-arranged rendezvous. But where? Our only hope for their capture lay in attempting to follow some of them, and then, by keeping the various observed courses plotted on the space charts, eventually figuring out where, approximately, that rendezvous lay in all the infinite reaches of space. That blasting off in a variety of directions was a clever maneuver—one they had accomplished smoothly and at inimitable speed—and a precision that bespoke much dangerous practice in the zones of weightlessness.

I had flung the Darkome into that center of neutralized gravities between two spatial bodies and pushed the lever controlling the dis-flows to the driver plates. Rammed it home to the last notch, swinging the ship with short side bursts, jockeying the craft to conform with the zig-zag swings of the pursuit needle, following the crooked trail of the gas ions left hanging in the ether by the force flows from the driver-plates of the Satanists' ships.

Somewhere ahead, the enemy flung himself deeper into the evernight of space. My ionic-indicator—a device to pick up the most tenuous of ion trails (standard equipment on all the battle ships of Nor) had finally stopped its wild gyrations and held steady on what was an ionic trail dead ahead. This was it! No more of the excitement and doubt if we would get a trail that wasn't just a decoy—this was heavy with the exhaust of a large craft—steady enough to indicate that the ship or ships just ahead were actually going some place. And, if the speed that we were making was any indication of just how fast the enemy was going, he was really racing through space at close to the top acceleration of the Darkome—the Darkome that I had worked and studied over and had the crew tune until it had the reputation as one of the fastest ships in the Nortan fleet. But, then, it should be—the best mechanical minds in my planet had been building it for three centuries.

Like the thoroughbred that she was, the Darkome settled down to the chase . . . the scent of the quarry was in her mechanical nostrils—and her powerful drivers were capable of hurtling her to the infinity of spatial boundaries if need be. We would catch whatever was ahead of us if it took years at this terrific speed.

Somewhere ahead that enemy crew bored a hole ever deeper into speed blackened space, their drivers heating as those of the Darkome were heating. Where would the chase lead?

Footnotes

1   This "universal viewer" is a device which assembles and coordinates the images resulting from a large number of penetray beams and their accompanying televisor—or direct-view screens. These beams point to every direction in space and the screen images are reprojected upon tiny mental vision (telaug) beams directly into the brain of the pilot of the ship. (Telaug beams carry mental messages in a large part of the communication system of the Nortans.) The result was a complete mental view in all directions disturbing to a man used to seeing in but one direction at a time. But to a pilot accustomed to the device, it was a vastly superior method to the older devices—which gave a single view of the space directly ahead. They were standard equipment on all Nortan war-craft of any size. With it, an experienced pilot is continuously conscious of the contents of space in every direction simultaneously—and could at the same time use his exterior vision for other purposes, to write a report—or a letter home.—Author.

2   DEFECTION: Note the persistence of this word—WITH the meaning INTACT—"dis-integrant energy infection," is shortened to DEfection, and STILL means—"to fall into evil; err on a job."—Author.

3   ZONE OF WEIGHTLESSNESS: In a place where no thing has weight, infinite acceleration can be achieved with every slight impetus—no inertia drag would crush the occupants. The acceleration would have no effect on the bodies of the passengers.

   A 'zone of weightlessness'—neutralized gravity—exists between any two bodies in space. These zones would be used by space ships as starting points for all long, fast voyages.—Author.

CHAPTER II.

WHENCE CAME SATHANAS?

This Arch-Angle, Sathanas, is not of the race of Nor. Being of Earth myself, it pains me to say that his ancestors first breathed the then untainted air of the third planet. Sathanas sprang from a vari-form family, originating among the Angles of Earth, which we call Mu. The Angles had originally been a blond, blue-eyed family of normal-appearing Earthmen. Then, some time in the past, Sathanas' bloodline had been crossed with some dark, hairy, cloven-hooved race of space. Long before the migration which emptied most of the Sun's planets of intelligent life, his family had taken over a dark planet—by name, Satana—on the outer rims of the Nor Empire. In time, their ability had won them the administration of the affairs of the planet from the Rulers of Nor. And, from that one planet, eventually, they were given the Rulership of all the little planets in the small system of which Satana was the dominant world. The "Angles" and their leaders were variously designated—a separate political group under their "Monitor Angles—Arch-Angles—and their supreme head, their Ruler and representative in the God Council on Nor—Elder Angle Fontal.

There were some dozen of the Arch-Angles with some dozen small planets in their administration. One of these was the Arch-Angle Sathanas, Ruler of the Home planet of the Angles in their group, the planet Satana. Being the first planet that the family had settled on after they left Mu, they had, in accordance with the customs of the God-Race, taken the name of the planet that they ruled as their family name. The rest of these planets were colonized with Angles from the cities of Earth . . . a numerous, systemwide clan.

Sathanas' family had been well liked for a long time . . . and being just and wise rulers, they, as well as the peoples under them, prospered. And so, Sathanas had the best education that Nor could provide.

As I remember Sathanas, he was a fellow of some fifty feet in height, dark visaged, with the horns that indicated a crossing of the blood line with that of some Titans (which wasn't uncommon in ancient Mu) . I had seen him first at a council meeting some centuries ago, when I first acquired the status of a Ruler by my acquisition of the tiny planet of Callay. It was after concluding most of the formal ceremony incidental to the investiture of several new rulers that someone first introduced us.

I can still picture the scene as he first greeted me with the accepted ceremony of Nor's tradition. A score of usLemurians, Titans, Atlans, variforms and a few from planets I'd never heard of—had found the favor of the Elders of the Council of Nor and were being made rulers of certain planets of the Nor Empire. Not big, important planets, true . . . but still, we were all pleased that we should be so honored by the Elders. Not all became rulers as they grew older and bigger—even of small planets and planetoids.

Finally, the long ceremonies of creating a new ruler of a provincial planet were over and we could relax for a brief time before the festivities began in celebration of the event. Several of us newly invested rulers had gathered together slightly apart from the tremendous bulk of swarming Elders—gathered in a laughing, harmlessly excited little circle. We kept congratulating one another and with mock solemnity addressed each other with all the titles we'd ever heard and remembered. That was one of the best moments of my life. I recall that I laughed, and raising my right arm in a formal Nortan salute, had addressed a great golden-haired Titan, though he was one of us, addressed him with as solemn a look and as impressive voice as I could manage.

"O Mighty Zeus, Grand Lord of the Thirtieth Tender Fleet, Conqueror of Limitless Cow Pastures, Ruler of the Lately Discovered World of Olympia, Greetings! Grant . . ."

"My Lords!" At the strange sound of someone addressing us so, we turned startled and looked up into the smiling understanding eyes of one of the Elders of Nor—one of the younger ones. He couldn't have been more than a few centuries older than we. For a moment we didn't know what to say, but the Elder continued before we became embarrassed.

"My Lords, may I present the Lord Sathanas, Arch-Angle and Ruler of the Planet Satana?"

We returned his salute and noticed this 'Lord Sathanas' that he'd presented. Accustomed as I am to life in all its varied forms and colors, the dark, ominous appearance of 'Lord Sathanas' was slightly depressing. He was too dark. Not the bronze darkness of a heavy space tan but the darkness of the sky just before a storm on Mother Mu. He made no effort to be friendly, just greeted us with stock phrases as though impatient to meet people more his equal. His impatience and boredom were further emphasized by the way he kept prancing on his cloven hooves—his heritage from some variform ancestor—and by the nervous way he kept drumming his fingers on the jeweled clasp of his weapon belt. Nothing about him pleased me, particularly the swaggering way he kept his long dark cape in motion. I thought to myself, 'What's he afraid of—that we'll contaminate his precious cloak?' I looked him full in the face—that handsome cynical face with the blue eyes of his Angle family, icily and incongruously staring back at me with the disdain ill-befitting a Ruler of Nor. That struck me as odd and jarring, here in this usually solemn hall(and my nostrils twitched with the scent of the evil, sulphurous odor about him, no doubt from some ingredient of his nutrient vapors.

I should have known then, or at least have been suspicious, but, in the hallowed halls of the Council of Nor one does not suspect one's equals. But he was a dero [4]—I know that now.

There was a time, once, when the peoples of Mu and the other Sun planets were unaware that there could be such a thing as a dero. But that was when the Sun and Earth were young—before the Sun burned hot and deadly. But as the Sun burned down through its layers of carbon, it eventually reached the heavier substances near its core—the "de"—producing radio-active metals. It is the deadly emanations given off by burning radio-actives that produce in life, a dero—a detrimental energy from the Sun that so motivates life that they are like that which is robot—controlled by these "de", or detrimental energy emanations—evil completely.

We didn't find that out until later, though. His family, foolishly indulgent, had concealed all the signs of his deroism. They didn't know enough of science to realize what a dread thing a dero can be.

They had paid for their indulgence and their ignorance with their lives—lives that should have been immortal—for the first of Sathanas crimes had been the summary and permanent removal of all the heirs above his rank in the family blocking his mad rise to power.

'Something has happened to Sathanas', people said. In a way, they were right, but they didn't know in what way or they would have removed him. I know from similar cases that his character was a long time growing.

Sathanas had been born on the planet Mu (Earth) in one of the older cities and the mech of that city was condemned not long after Sathanas had left Mu to become the satellite Ruler of one of the planets under the Elders of Nor.

His was pretty much the same background, in many ways, as that of Ex-Elder Zeit whose antecedents I had studied long ago, as I had been curious as to how an apparently intelligent man had become such an unthinking monster.

I thought—and experiments of the Elder scientists subsequently proved—that aging mech has produced many a criminal. I think that their subjection to the infected energy from the wornout pleasure mech was the cause of this as it formed their inner polarization—their very soul—along dis-inductive lines. Hence, as long as stars blaze in space, such characters will induct that will to Evil from the stars' mighty destructive fields. And unfortunately there is absolutely no way to prevent these creations.

The whole group connected with Sathanas had fallen into some evil and dissipated habits, had formed a cult of great power, and had built secret hideouts where they could indulge their perverted tastes in safety. They did not relish being deterred by Nor laws protecting the rights of every individual to safety of person. All this evil they had kept concealed behind many a barrier of sub-officials. And all went along smoothly for the Gods of Space know only how many years.

But finally, a very beautiful young Nor maiden had wheedled and vamped her way out of their unholy clutches and exposed the whole rotten mess.

Their use of girls for wall ornaments, [5] living in stimmed nutrient, the whole depraved business of torture for pleasure and profit—the horrible circuses where captive men were forced to fight for their lives against beasts from the unsettled sun-planets—all this disgusting blight on the rule and culture of the Nor Empire had finally been dragged out into the open. What Sathanas had thought was a corner on illegal entertainment had turned into a trap from which he was now just barely making his escape.

Footnotes

4   DERO: (See 'I Remember Lemuria")
5   STIMMED BODY—ORNAMENTS: This use of girls and women for ornaments is a particularly revealing angle on the opulence and cruel disregard for the natural rights of man which has marked ray-secrets since the earliest days. This use is an old, and still extant, custom in the caverns that honeycomb this planet we call Earth but which the ancient ancestors of all of us called Mu. Down there in the great old ray mansions' salons are wall brackets where young women are hung, and the stim currents of too great pleasure flows make their bodies rigid with an overwhelming synthetic nerve-electric. The

effect is one of great beauty for the girls' young bodies are then like forced flowers pouring out all the beauty and love of a lifetime in an almost visible and very sensual outpouring of energy—like the flower pours out its pollen in a single day. Thus a place can be decorated with human flowers—if one doesn't care how soon such human flowers wilt. When the custom began, it is probable that the wonderful old mech contained strong beneficial flows which made the experience of the human ornament one of benefit. They survived, stronger than before and better. But as the mech grows older, such strong subjections to great energy flows from the old mech are no longer supportable by the human frame.

In the caverns, the custom still survives of decorating the walls for a feast with these living stimmed ornaments, but the custom of surviving the ordeal of pleasure has perished, from what I hear.—Author.

CHAPTER III.

BACK ON MOTHER MU

The great sensitive needles of the ionic-trail-indicator [6] became still and fell back against the pin marked 'O'—no more trail.

In the split second that the needle stopped, I leaped to my feet, stabbing the button opening the ship communicator.

"All hands! Attention! Reverse drivers! View screen open! Gun crews stand by!"

The great dreadnor braked to a tortured halt from full velocity. I could hear Tyron taking over control, alerting the crew for battle—action that might start immediately. Barked orders maneuvered the ship's immense bulk into the exact center of the "zone of weightlessness".

"—we might have to move fast."

"Where are we?" I asked myself, as soon as I had made sure that the enemy wasn't in the neighborhood.

"This constellation looks familiar," I mused. "Can it be . . . still . . . it is!"

Opening the communicator, I called, "Arl! Do you recognize that planet in your view screen? It's Mu!" Nostalgia gripped me. A homesickness I didn't think I could still feel smothered me at the sight of the familiar seas and green, white-topped mountains of my abandoned homeland of almost two thousand years ago.

Taking over the controls from the pilot who didn't even suspect that the planet under us was my former home, I tooled the mighty Darkome to a landing on Mu's satellite. For all of her tremendous mass, she slid gently to a stop in the glistening, liquid-air snow sheltered by the black shadow of one of the moon's mountains.

I ordered the tender broken out, then called to the control room.

"I am going to take Lady Arl to the surface of this satellite's planet. While I am scouting down there, keep the crew alerted."

Tyron saluted, looking a bit envious—envy, I guess, at the thought that he wasn't going to see his desired action. "Yes, sir," was all he said.

"Observe standard precautions for operation in enemy territory. Avoid using equipment as much as possible to cut down the chances for detection."

"Yes, sir," he nodded.

"I don't know where the Sathanas' ship or ships have gone, but I doubt if they would be apt to be close by and still be undetected by our mech. But, until you hear from me, take no chances. That's an order!"

Returning his salute, the Lady Arl, who had come to the control room, and I boarded the tender and took off. And not too comfortably, either. A tender is a small spacer for short flights—lifeboats for the crew, and on the Darkome the tenders were big, but two thousand years of Vanue's wizardy of growth had increased our height till we were well over fifty feet.

Both Arl and I felt the old excitement we'd experienced as youths using the small spacers for picnics from Mu to the Moon—felt excitement as I drove the little craft to the surface of the doomed planet for the first visit in a score of centuries.

Our excitement soon turned to sadness. This wasn't the same planet we'd left—no darting ships—no shining towers—no signs of civilized life.

"Oh, Mion," spoke the lovely Arl beside me, "this is all so sad and unreal. I feel like—Mion! Look! What's that over there?"

"It looks like . . . it is a city, Arl!" Her enthusiasm was contagious. "Shall we go over there?"

"Oh, yes, Mion. Let's see what man has done in all these years."

"All right, Arl, but remember we are not allowed to stay here long."

She nodded, silent.

We of the Nor are not allowed to stay long on a sunlit planet, for one's character soon becomes twisted—not necessarily into evil, but certainly into err—which can be worse. One in err is stupidly convinced of his correctness, of his own brilliance. All of our food and drink must be brought from our ship, for the radioactives in the water and meat of Earth may not be eaten by Nor men by law. That err, that mental polarization, is the thing men of Earth must fight most fiercely, for err will live in their thinking, an illogic that will make them think black is white till they are forced to check the question with a colorimeter.

We would pay for my stay on this sad planet with many boring hours before the medicos finish the mental tests to make sure that we have not been seriously affected by the sun's hard light. Sometimes I believed they feared evil and its cause too much to fight it effectively. The old medicos can be tiresome themselves, to the point of evil. I would like to give some of them a few tests myself—of my own devising. Yes! They are too close to some dense metals—err magnets of another kind—and have become polarized by the dullest and heaviest metal to be found on a thousand master-size planets, that I know.

I expected to stay but the few hours allowed me and then away. Nearly two thousand years of the destructive magnetic field sweep of the sun had passed over old Mu. The difference between this little planet third from the Sun and the dark planets is immense. There, time is a growth, never a loss. Here, time is a sorrow, a slow destruction, a completely OPPOSITE QUANTITY. Here, the proud towers of Old Atlantis are crumbling stones, eroded by the blowing sands of the encroaching deserts that did not exist under Atlan science. There, the fecund growth of man has multiplied the beauty and pleasure, the power and the glory of Nor, many, many times in these two thousand years.

Having seen death in many forms, I like to fight death's burning face wherever I find it. Surely, death's face is burning brighter on Mother Mu than on any other globe these feet have trod, feet that sink further into the dis-softened stones [7] of this planet than any other I know. Many have been the globes trod since I last left old Mu to voyage through the dark voids where no light but the light of wisdom can be found. Dull it is, to one who has tasted war and death, and swift-tiding battles, to speed on some mission in which the element of danger has been reduced to the undetectable minimum. I am a warrior, trained through many centuries of supremely difficult schooling to the rigors of battle and war, and there are few indeed, for Nor men to fight who even dare to think of braving our slightest displeasure.

Nearly two thousand years had passed since I distributed the records of the Atlan migration to dark space to guide the men who should come after us on Mu.

As I guided the craft in a hovering flight over the scarred face of old Mu, I marveled at the green growth over everything, for it is hard to realize that though everything dies of the Sun poisons, life goes on, renewed forever. After first coming upon such worlds of death, one cannot accustom oneself to the idea that all this life that looks so vibrant and virile is so short-lived.

I know that since I had left Mu, cities probably had grown and died upon her surface, and cities under her surface must have been peopled and have again lost their peoples in the wars that always rage on the sun-burned planets.

Arl and I glided over the glittering golden roofs of the city, and, settling to Earth some miles distant, entered a cavern whose ancient shafts still gaped, unfilled by the rubble that now choked most of the openings to the Elder world. We were anxious to see what life had taken root within the caverns, for there lay the tools of the ancient wisdom, waiting for a wise man-child's learning. Arl opened the great air lock at the bottom of the shaft and I floated the tender in to the floor of the cavern.

We fell to rummaging about in the ruins of the great mansions, as one will in these old places. I activated one of the penetray view rays and took a look at the shining city on the surface not far away. A one man flier of an antique make rose from the city and came toward us. I augmented the passengers' mind, saw that his name was Tyr, that he was of the Aesir, as the people of the city evidently called themselves. He had seen our ship and was coming to investigate. He seemed excited, as though something about our appearance had revealed to him that we were the uncommon "visitors from the stars" mentioned in the legends and folk-tales of his people.

"Arl," I called to my lovely lady who was busy satisfying her curiosity about some of the old mechanisms at the far wall of this big room. "Arl, come here and watch this flier—he seems to be heading this way!"

With the quick, cat-like change of interest of women, Arl pranced gaily over to where I sat at the controls of the tele-thought augmentor. With a pleased little laugh, she wagged that ever-charming tail of hers and took her place beside me.

As we sat at the screen watching the approaching flier, we could see his mind was a maelstrom of conflicting sentiments—I couldn't repress my laughter at the fear I saw there. But there are times when Arl saves me from unrequired cruelty, and when I laughed, she chided me.

"Oh Mion, don't laugh at that poor little man! Remember, it has been almost twenty centuries since they have had a visit from any of the Elder Races."

"Lovely Arl," I agreed, "I had forgotten. I should have remembered that fear goes with sun-infection."

"He is a brave man, Mion," Arl pointed out. "He is afraid, yet his will to investigate makes him overcome his fear. If he is representative of mankind . . .

I nodded, knowing what Arl meant. As long as there are brave men on Earth who can conquer their fear and dread with their own wills, there is hope that mankind can, in time, defeat the "de" curse of the Sun.

"Look, Mion, he's dropping down the shaft as though he has done it many times before."

It was true. The pilot of the little flier expertly dropped down the shaft and came to rest beside the Darkome's tender. There was a moment of indecision—Arl and I knew from reading his mind that it was all he could do to restrain a wild, nearly uncontrollable impulse to flee. He took heart, however, stepped from his machine, and came toward us. He was large for the race of Earthmen, being about twelve feet high.

Finally, eyes bulging, he stood in awe before us where we sat at the ancient mech.

I greeted him by name: "Ho, Tyr, what brings you to us who are strangers to you?"

At that he flung himself prostrate before us. Our lack of enmity loosed his tongue and he protested: "Of course you know me, O Gods from the Stars. I have heard the old men speak of your kind, and have read something of you in the ancient writings, but many of us no longer believe in the greater Gods. Of course, you understand all mysteries, and you have read my thoughts over the ancient mechanisms I see you toying with. I am of the Aesir race, and that is our city you see in the distance. I am one of the few who understand the great significance of your coming here. Odin, our all-father, in his palace invites your presence. We have great need of your wisdom, Mighty Ones."

I finally assented to Tyr's importuning and the invitation of Odin himself over the great ray called Odin's Eye, and we entered the tender and took off for the palace of Gladsheim [8] dominating the shining, gilded-roofed city of Asgard in the distance.

We spiralled down toward the great courtyard of the palace, reading a dozen minds on my telaug on the way down.

It is habitual for a Nor to be careful. There was nothing but curiosity and awe in their minds; this was no trap, I knew. As I landed the ship, several brawny, armored warriors came up to us. Axes were slung on their belts beside the antique dis-ray pistols, pistols of a type that the science of the high gods has not surpassed to this day. They spoke the ancient universal tongue called Mantong, but time had so changed the pronunciation that it was difficult to understand it at once. We used small portable telaugs to tell what was in the minds about us anyway. We easily carried them in our hands. But Arl and I soon began fully to understand the speech, for the basic sounds were all the same as our own, and not by any means are we mentally slow.

To our way of thinking, these Aesir were little fellows. They were not more than ten or twelve feet in height. The largest showed the graying hair of age, the sign dreaded most of all plagues, in all space, caused from over exposure to the poisonous emanations of a deadly Sun. In space flight, sometimes it happens that some poorly plotted course flashes a ship close into the terrible heat and deadly particles of the field surrounding some dense sun. Also, sometimes, in the little time of their passing such a sun at light speed, their hair grows white, and they die in a few weeks. Such is impregnation by radio-active particles—sure death. Old Sol, the Earth's sun, is not that bad, but it, too, is sure death. A great pity arose in me that these fine men did not know what caused their age, or how to avoid it if they did know. This pity of mine is one reason some man will sometime find this record I leave, and know how to shun the terrible plague of space, the deadly, dense particles from heavy suns that get into the flesh and stay, burning away good life force and leaving a shrivelled corpse.

Do you remember the lovely Arl? She is still Arl, but grown so big now that the Mutan who loved her then would worship at her feet as once he worshipped at Vanue's huge beauty ... for that matter I still do anyway. She is here beside me now, toying with the ancient stim rays; the stim ray that is forbidden as its effects can be most evil if the metal is too far gone in slow disintegrance. But Arl carries with her a meter of my devising containing a dial which reveals the most minute flows of "de" force dangerous to man.

She must know if this one is dangerous stim or not. It seems to be still usable, for a vastly pleasurable viray is flowing over my form even now from her hands, and her soft lips are multiplied a laughing million of times all over me. I am forever startled by the endlessly varied stim augments that Arl's infinite wit finds in any mech of the kind. I have had a billion tiny Arls lift me in my sleep and carry me to Elysia, their forms growing more and more about me, till all the world was soft, gleaming, rosy Arl, the flowers her faces, the breeze from her lips, and the stim rays looks from her eyes, loving me, while her hair became a vast forest of titanic, curling beauty sheltering me in its scented shade.

There are no words or images to tell you what a girl of imagination can do with stim augments of her thought. I still think of Arl as a girl, and she looks like a girl, too, except her size is as great as my own, and that is too much to think about. For soon we must leave our loved home on Nor and move on to the heavier planets [9] of the Elder cities, and that is a hard time for adjustment, as it takes years to accustom oneself to the great gravity.

Footnotes

6   GAS IONS: While the driver flow is a kind of reverse gravity formed by the disintegration of a certain metalloy, during the expansion under the discurrent, much gas is formed exclusive of the integrative snapback flow of exd which is the frictional flow forming the drive. The dissociating sub-atoms of the driver plates pass through a gaseous stage where they leave a trail that is detectable. This ionizing trail is an unavoidable product of this form of drive.—Author.

7   One of the most repeated legends of the Gods coming again to Earth is the detail that their heavy feet sank ankle deep into solid rock—a very interesting legend—heavy-planet races denoted.—Author.

8   Note that this city of Asgard and this Gladsheim are not the city or people mentioned in the story "Thought Records of Lemuria," but is a city which takes its name from the site of one of the first cities built by the Atlans.

These Aesir are the latter gods who take many of their names from the elder gods; cities are named in the same manner.—Author.

9. HEAVIER PLANETS: At a certain point in their development, the Normen must leave home and go to the heavier planets for development. They do not return from these heavy planets to the lighter ones except as rulers or teachers. The princess Vanue and the other very tall characters appearing in these stories have returned to the children races as teachers, rulers, or judges. All the Elders are of this class of returned people.—Author.

CHAPTER IV.

PACT WITH THE AESIR

Odin welcomed us himself, leading us into the great hall of Gladsheim. The walls were covered with the gleaming shields of his followers; he sat us upon his own throne and the throne of his queen beside it. They were the only seats that could begin to hold us, for they were relics from the old time and must have been too great for their present users. So we took them, and indeed, Arl and I are used to great honor wherever we go, for we are much loved and respected. "A friend is the best gold," is my motto, and can be a mighty power when he is needed.

As he stood before us, Odin was nearly half our height. But age was showing on him. His beard was snow white, his ruby-red Santa Claus face lined with the progress of the dreaded sun-blight.

Odin stood on the steps of the throne dais and made a short speech to his followers.

"These are the high Gods who live among the far stars. You have heard of them from our wise men, and now they are here for you to see. They come at a time when we need them most. If they approve of us, our struggles with the Jotuns will go well, so hold your evil natures in check, and let the High Gods see the gold that we, your friends and I your ruler, know lies underneath the rude flesh." Then Odin turned to us, saying:

"We know much of your ancient race from writings found in the caves—the plates of imperishable metal left by Mutan Mion have been translated by some of our wise men, and I have read their writings. Also, we have learned to use some of the ancient magic from the hot depths of the greater caverns where a man can no longer live for the heat. There we have found great things and brought them to the surface for use here in Gladsheim. We would like to have you explain many things about that science that produced such things, but just now we are getting ready for a seige. The Jotuns are preparing for an attack on Asgard. Even now their hosts gather in the misty depths of the dark land beyond. What are your names that I may properly present you to our brave warriors?"

With a bow toward Arl, I said, "This is the Lady Arl and I am called Mion."

Arl smiled at them with the graciousness of a true queen.

"My Lord is too modest," she said in that lovely voice. "He is the Lord Mutan Mion, the Lord Mion to whom even the Elder Titans and Atlans owe their lives."

The Aesirs' eyes popped with surprise and joy when they heard that we were the same Mutan Mion and Arl mentioned on the ancient plates.

"So many lives . . . and still living," were their excited comments, "so long . . . and so young to look upon. So fair, and yet so ancient of days. Yea, they are the Gods . . . come again to Earth as in the old days that some swear were true things."

But Odin had little time for much formality, though he seemed to think we merited a great deal of it.

"Oh Great Ones from Beyond, if you will not help us against the Jotuns, we must leave you for awhile and get to our work, preparing to meet the coming attack, but, Oh Mighty Ones, if you will help us, we are yours. Command us what we must do to beat off the fierce Jotuns."

As he spoke a messenger raced into the hall. With some urgency he approached the dais that held the throne and spoke privately into Odin's ear. The worthy human's face fell. As he turned again to us, I could detect a note of sadness in his voice.

"The messenger brings bad news, My Lords. Another great ship from the stars—infinitely larger than the one in which you arrived—has come to Earth in the encampment of the Jotuns. That is not the whole of this ill news. Mighty men of a size as your own have come out of this huge vessel and are siding with the Jotuns in their preparation for the coming struggle with us. What means that to you, O Great Beings?"

Now, I knew that there was but one Nor ship in this immediate solar system, and that another space ship as large as the Darkome probably was the fugitive that we were seeking—one of the ships of the infamous fleet we were pledged to return to the Courts of the Rulers of Nor. I explained to these Earthmen that these were fugitives from the justice of the Gods, and that I could summon power to crush them utterly, as soon as I contacted my ship, the Darkome.

"Are the Jotuns and these strangers in view ray range?" I asked the white-bearded Odin.

"They smugly think they are not," was his answer as he led me to the instrument called "Odin's Eye." [10] It was really a vast space telescope with a tri-dimensional screen, a big box of luminous mist in which three dimensional pictures of the objects in focus could be seen. Within it we saw the gathering place of the Jotuns, and monsters they were, recently having come to Earth from some huge, colder planet. There, their size had been naturally determined by the conditions of the planet. They were three times the size of the Aesir, [11] of a greater size than Odin himself, and infinitely uglier than any others I have ever seen. I had heard of the Jotuns, an evil race shunned by all wise men. They had a custom of following up Atlan and Titan migrations and occupying their abandoned cities for the pleasure instruments which were always to be found in the abandoned pleasure palaces and mansions of the immortals. They were, consequently, not entirely unaccustomed to handling ray equipment, and would prove mean antagonists for the Aesir. The Aesir had had many a brush with them since their arrival a century ago, and had come off a too close first in most of them.

Obviously, the Aesir were not relishing the contemplation of a war to the last ditch between the two races, for the Jotuns were not only more numerous, but they had occupied and used more of the ray equipment-filled caves than the Aesir. The Aesir ignorantly chose to build their cities on the surface in the cheerful sunlight, and they did not understand what the Sun did to them. A few of their wise men had warned them of the writings left by the Gods which told them that the Sun caused old age, but they scoffed at this as old men's garrulous fear. The only ray the Aesir had was portable equipment they had laboriously brought to the surface for their use.

When I saw the huge, dark figure of Sathanas himself among them, I knew several things by swift deduction. First, I knew his presence here was no accident. Second, I knew that here was the rendezvous of the fleeing ships the patrol had pursued to all the points of the compass, for it was not likely that Sathanas would have had time to mix into the quarrels of the Jotuns unless he was waiting here for that rendezvous. And last, I knew that Sathanas had had dealings with these gigantic and hideous Jotuns before to know them so well. Such dealings were forbidden expressly by law. The Elder Race literally 'fathered' the human race and they made strict laws protecting the lives of their children. The Jotuns were well known as slave dealers, [12] and what was worse, they were known for their modifications on the ancient mechanisms they salvaged from abandoned caverns—modifications which made the mech potent tools for the changing of good human character to evil ends.

Putting a telaug beam on Sathanas' head in the tridimensional screen, I heard his thought and from it I gathered a general impression corroborating my deductions. For centuries, he had traded and had been in communication with these Jotuns. This was also forbidden by the Nor laws. For a long time he sold them Nor maids for slaves, and in return, he received much illegal equipment which the Jotuns manufactured from the ancient pleasure mech. It was evident that he had long ago promised them aid against the Aesir in return for some favor. That his flight from the Nor wrath was unknown to the Jotuns was clear, for he was striving with all his mighty brain to keep the knowledge of his trouble from escaping to their minds over the telaug over which the conference was being conducted. Evidently he did not intend to risk his ship in the coming battle, but was seated at a great table in the gloomy ruined home which was their meeting place, going over their battle plans with the leaders. These leaders were a fearful lot to look upon. Though somewhat lacking in logical mental powers, they seemed to make up for this by fierceness of physique and ruthlessness of intent.

Gathered in the vast cave that stretched its murky depths into the hidden distance were the sons of Loki and Sigyn, the wife of Loki. How he ever came to marry her was too much for me, for she was many times his size and as evil visaged as hell itself. The witch, Hela, who was not Loki's daughter, and who had no regard for him, was a very tall giantess of a hideous whiteness like frost, or dead bones. Evil lived in her eyes and on her face, and on her face twisted a shadow of death. Like most devotees of the spirit of evil, she was obviously mad and possessed of a mad-woman's peculiar appetites, augmented and exaggerated as they so easily can be by the use of the beneficial and stim. Also, there were many leaders of the Jotuns, hairy, gray beast-men, thirty feet high, knotted muscles, and armed with every kind of weapon known to two civilizations—stone clubs hung side by side with flame swords of a make superior to any made now, for the art is a lost one. This horde knew ray work, and they were blood-thirsty fighting men proved in a thousand brawls and dozens of wars. The Aesir had cause to worry, for these were professional warriors brought from space for the express purpose of getting the powerful Aesir out of the way for their commerce in souls, slaves and perverting mech. Evidently this was the reason Sathanas was here, as this commerce of the Jotuns was his greatest single source of income. The Aesir had a bad habit of raiding the Jotun's strongholds and releasing the poor human beasts.

But the Einheriar, [13] the chosen, the warriors of Odin, were no match in size or in experience for this bunch of mad dogs from the pleasure dens of a dozen planets.

I doubted that this affair would ever come to hand to hand combat. I looked down into Odin's great "eye" for a chance to find out just what range weapons were available to the Horde, what they planned to use immediately. Sathanas was talking.

"All this array of armed force is of no use. One long range ray brings the whole army to naught. We must have a spy, someone who can tell us just what range weapons they have to use against us."

Loki pushed his comparatively small form to the foreground, shouting, "The Aesir have no weapons worth worrying about. I knew every ray in Asgard. They cannot touch us. You can sweep the whole place clean of life with one ray from your mighty ship."

I turned to Odin, "Just what is the range of your weapons?" I asked him.

"I can't reach him," answered Odin.

"I can see him, but I can't hit him."

"You don't know much about these tri-dimensional screens, I am afraid, O All-Father. Let me show you something."

Pulling a side arm from my belt, I directed its epileptoray pencil at Sathanas' head in the cube-screen, Sathanas immediately curled up into an agonized, crumpled heap of writhing, shrieking, slobbering flesh. The table, surrounded by the gigantic Jotuns, and a few of the really gigantic cohorts of Sathanas, leaped to their feet, mouths gaping in astonishment.

"See, Father, the beam of this particular view ray is constructed to transmit energy complete, and is, consequently, a most efficient and adaptable weapon, ready to carry any energy to any point it reaches, and it has tremendous penetrative range, as you can see. Some of this type of ray will even dislodge furniture, or transmit the energy of a push. Watch!" I seized a war club from the wall. It was very small for me, like a child's toy hammer in my hands, and I tapped one of the heads of the Sathanists. [14] He promptly dropped unconscious or dead to the floor. "You see, you didn't know what there was in this beam. It is a very fine example of the best work of that particular time."

Odin waited for no prompting from me, but seized a club from the wall and started bopping every head in the ray screen. Regularly I moved the beam a little to keep a good bunch of the enemy within its slightly reduced vision, reduced from life size, and pencilled my own epileptic-ray at everyone of the misfits of life that I could reach. Odin was enjoying himself immensely, and we had nearly cleared the cavern of its hundred or so big-shots of the Jotuns when a huge black shorter-ray swung out of Sathanas' vast ship from dark space and grounded Odin's Eye. Odin's fun was over for the time, his beam shorted to the ground by the black conductor ray. His troubles with the super science Sathanas had brought from his Nor-governed home had just begun. So had all Earthmen's troubles with Sathanas.

I figured that Odin's bopping of Jotun pates would have the effect of holding off the attack until I had time to make ready for it, because they hadn't known that they could be reached. I radioed the Darkome for certain supplies and for certain technicians I would need. Why didn't I tell them to radio a Nor base and tell them of the whereabouts of Sathanas? Because I had an idea that I could take Sathanas apart with a device I was planning to construct, and that I could bring him in single-handed, which would be quite a feather in my cap. Such is a man's thought when near a sun. Always wrong. It was foolish to do without the help I could have acquired so quickly, but I thought it a splendid idea, and so original. I had never had such a wonderful idea before. Err is very deluding when it appears in a mind unaccustomed to it.

First I asked the Aesir for a list of every available ray device within the city. When I got the list, I checked off the types of ray I wanted—those with a good long beam that would carry the greatest amount of superimposed power, and those with the most potent destructive qualities, regardless of the range. The latter would be aided in carrying power by the former in the huge device I was planning for the downfall of Sathanas. Why didn't I call the Darkome to me? I had another err—the less equipment I used to capture Sathanas, the greater would be my glory. Such errs I might have corrected if I had been used to their presence in my mind, but in the clean magnetic fields of Nor planets one's thought is naturally correct and I was unprepared for the sudden flood of distorted ideas the Sun was releasing in my mind.

On the list of ray equipment brought me, there were all kinds of pleasure rays and healing rays, but few weapon rays. The pleasure and healing rays were tricky stuff, well built, some of it, but of little use in a battle except for observation, inspiring the fighters, or for healing the wounded. I knew that Sathanas' black cruiser was loaded to its capacity with the heaviest war-ray available which was, as I know now, a power unsurveyed by any law-abiding eyes. So, it was hard to say just what he might have up his sleeve in the way of fighting ray. Whether his fleet would rendezvous with him here on Earth, or whether he was to meet them elsewhere, I could not make sure, for his trained mind had felt my probing thought and doubled the answer—saying that both were true. I suspected that the first was the truth and that we would have hundreds of outlaw ships flaming down upon us at any moment. Sathanas seemed committed to supporting the Jotuns in return for their cooperation in his own plans. Sathanas' crew on his ship kept the black shorterbeam on our view-beam, and Odin's Eye was the only ray of master size in the city. We had no way of knowing now what they were up to. Principally, I was anxious to know whether any of the other ships of Sathanas had joined him or not.

This life on Earth is distorted and fading, a once brilliant picture that long ago fell on the water of life, and is now melting away. There is little left of the old God picture of life. The soft rounded chins of the Aesir young, the honest, beautiful truth in the undis-affected eyes of a child, the turned, beautiful perfection of some young limbs, these are the only true images left from the God era. The rest is distorted by an ill wind across the mirroring pool of life force. And thus it was that I saw those monstrous forms across the deep of Jotunheim, the life force distorted by some evil willed wind from Elvidnir—from the Hall of Hela in Niflheim—distorted and dying into the mental err of evil life.

While we waited for the supplies from the Darkome or for the arrival of the patrol ships from space, I put the Aesir at the construction of a cumbrous device I had seen put to good use on the field of battle. It was most effective, but slow to handle. It was a monstrous turntable, the axis of which was a universal joint. Throwing this piece of equipment together with the odds and ends available took two days of hard labor. Then we piled on it every ray device of destructiveness or ionizing power (to make the air a conductor for the other beams) that could be obtained in the whole city. The rays were then carefully aligned to throw a multi-beam of immense, irresistible power. Nothing of a portable nature could be possessed by the enemy to equal its vast power. The turntable took up the whole courtyard of the palace of Gladsheim, about the size of two city blocks. On the turntable, piled two and three deep, were rays of every type developed by the past Atlan and Titan life on Earth. I did not think that the Jotuns would have anything of the kind. In the center of this motley assemblage of destruction, I placed a small but very powerful dissociator of modern make I had brought from the Darkome.

Footnotes

10   ODIN'S EYE: Was this the origin of the legends regarding 'Odin's Eye'? Norse folk-tales recounted it as an all seeing 'eye,' or all-seeing god-like power. This just might have been the result, or the USE of just such ancient mechanism or equipment as in this story—the view ray. The view ray, which the authors claim still exist in the ancient, God-built caverns, probably operated on a principle similar to a combination of present day radar and television. The television part of the ancient 'mech' operates, in any event, without the need for a transmitting station. The same way, for instance, that

your radio might pick up a conversation a few miles away without the need of a radio station 'sending.'

It is amazing when you consider that right beneath our feet this present day, and for untold centuries of the past, such equipment has lain idle and unused—except by a few degenerate tribes that somehow have lived there for all those years. It is the claim of the authors that the use of this marvelous equipment by these degenerates, or 'dero,' their 'tampering' with the lives of surface people, is the cause of most of our ill's and 'bad luck.'—Editor.

11 Again referring to the books of Charles Fort:

He quotes from the JOURNAL OF AMERICAN FOLK LORE, 17-203. viz, "Certain stone hatchets are said to have fallen from the heavens."

The authors pose the question: Are these stone axes that have been reported as having fallen from the heavens perhaps the crude 'side arms' of an uncultured race of 'esoteric ones' who have learned to fly the ancient cave-contained space craft, making inter-planetary flights, yet, of themselves. incapable of making any more mechanically advanced war weapons than crude stone hatchets that they have within historical times dropped from their flying space craft? The reference above is the report of South American Indians.

As to the possible 'size' of members of uncultured ones, read further in Fort's THE BOOK OF THE DAMNED:

(From NATURE, 30-)

May, 1884, the 27th, at Tysnas, Norway, a meteorite had fallen; that the turf was torn up at the spot where the object had been supposed to have fallen: two days later "a very peculiar stone" was found nearby. The description is—"in shape and size very like the fourth part of a large Stilton cheese." See the story for a description of the size of the Jotunds and then compute how large the stone heads of their war axes would have to be.

In the same work, Fort quotes from The Proc. Soc. of Antiq. of Scotland, 1-1-

That in a lump of coal from a mine in Scotland an "iron instrument" had been found.

Is this another indication of the extreme age of the human race?

Again from Fort: Notice of a stone axe, 17 inches long, 9 inches across broad end. (Proc. Soc. of Ants. of Scotland, 1-9-184.)

American ANTIQUARIAN, 18–

Copper axe from an Ohio mound; 22 inches; weight 38 pounds.
AMERICAN ANTHROPOLOGIST, n.s., 8-299.

Stone axe found at Birchwood. Wisconsin: 28 inches long, 14 inches wide, 11 inches thick, weight 300 pounds.

HUMAN FOOTPRINTS FOUND IN SANDSTONE, Near CARSON, NEVADA—EACH PRINT 18 to 20 inches LONG. (Amer. Jour. Sci., 3-26139)—Editor.

12 DISAPPEARANCES—SLAVERY: The authors are convinced that there have been many writers in the past and the present who either knew or suspected the existence of the caverns beneath the surface of the Earth, or that there was a power or a force or a race that was influencing the human race, usually for evil. The numerous legends of evil spirits, and good ones, too, tales of strange happenings, and strange disappearances. Charles Fort was one of those who came closest to guessing, or knowing the mysteries contained in the artificial cave world beneath this Earth's surface. He thought that we were 'fished for,' or that the possibility existed that we were fished for. For what purpose? Our facts are still too intangible on this count to say for certain whether we are really fished for at the present day. But if in the centuries past, there were races such as the Jotuns, trading in living humans—as slaves (or food?)—might they not still be extant? Before the reader dismisses this question with "ridiculous!" let him read any of the daily papers of the past few years, or the books of Charles Fort for literally thousands of unexplained 'disappearances.' People seen one moment and never again—even in the larger cities that are presumably well guarded.

If the reader lives near any of the country's large cities, he might call the Missing Persons' Bureau, if any, and get the LOCAL statistics on the annual number of disappearances that are not accounted for, or the number undetected. Then, figure out how many large cities there are in the whole nation.—Author.

13 EINHERIAR: This persistent legend of raising the dead for purposes of acquiring soldiers, slaves, etc. seems to come from the extreme potency of the antique beneficial ray. I, myself, have seen a boy of eight killed by a fiend from a distance with detrimental ray, raised again by his mother with beneficial ray at full strength. The fiend killed the boy three times in a period of four days, each time his mother revived or raised him again within a few minutes. There are many accounts of the potency of these rays. Even the

thuggee of India believe that their unseen backers can raise them from the dead if they are killed. It is very probably true that they are revived after a short time of death by this means. The Hindu ascetics who slit open their stomachs and let out their intestines with a knife, then push them back in to have the wound heal at once are the same kind of phenomena.—R. S. Shaver.

14   PRECISE ACCURACY OF ANCIENT WEAPONS: These ancient weapons were so accurate and so built for durability that perhaps they are the means by which certain phenomena have been actuated. Charles Fort, in his book, WILD TALENTS, says this:

"In the London newspapers, last orMarch, 1908, was told a story, which, when starting off, was called "what the coroner for South Northumberland described as the most extraordinary case that he had ever investigated." The story was of a woman, at Whitley Bay, near Blyth, England, who according to her statement, had foundher sister, burned to death on an unscorched bed. This was the equivalence of the old stories of 'spontaneous combustion of human bodies."

(I don't know what significance, if any, is in the spelling of "extraordin-RAY," but that is the precise way it is spelled on page 909, THE BOOKS of CHARLES FORT, WILD TALENTS, published for the Fortean Society by HENRY HOLT AND COMPANY, New York, 1941.)

ST. LOUIS GLOBE-DEMOCRAT, Dec. 16, 1889.—"In some mysterious way, a fire started in the mahogany desk in the center of the office of the Secretary of War, at Washington, D. C. Several official papers were destroyed, but it was said that they were of no especial value, and could be replaced. Secretary Proctor cannot understand how the fire originated, as he does not smoke, and keeps no matches about his desk." Taken from the BOOKS OF CHARLES FORT—WILD TALENTS—Page 911.

CHAPTER V.

WAR AGAINST THE JOTUNS

The huge multi-beam we aimed by turning and tilting the great turntable by windlasses upon which the noble muscles of the Aesir were expanded by the hundreds. It was slow, but it was inexorable destruction. I had never seen an energy screen or a shorter-fan that could stand against such an assemblage of ray, anywhere. I had great faith in my rude handiwork, for I had seen it used. The trick, of course, was to align the beams perfectly, to form a very dense, small beam of utter power. Carefully sighting the thing at the base of the big black shorter-beam from Sathanas' hidden ship which still held Odin's Eye in its grip, we tried out our multi-beam. The black beam disappeared in a blaze of incandescence like the fall of a meteor. Whether we had hit Sathanas' ship or not I didn't know, but I did know that one beam generator was burned out for good. A good omen! I took over Odin's Eye now that it was useful again, and calling instructions to Tyr over the telaug, he walked the great beam along the lines of waiting ships of the Jotuns, the assembled raytanks, supply piles and equipment they had gathered for the prosecution of a long seige of Asgard. Where the multi-beam struck, there was left nothing but a great smoking ditch in the ground, a ditch which had no bottom—as far as the eye could see. The destruction was nearing completion which would end the Jotun hopes of a long war. But, it was not great enough, for as the beam neared the Jotun aircraft, the whole fleet took to the air. They had seen that the beam was slow, and they figured they could avoid it by air maneuvers. Like a great funnel of fury, they rose from the mouth of the cavern and came on to attack, spreading out and sweeping down on Asgard.

The Jotuns—the personnel of the enemy—came from a dozen planets forgotten by the Atlans after their migrations. The Atlans were one of the greatest space roving races of all times, inhabiting thousands of dark, sunless planets and planetoids, a race that peopled a big chunk of outer space. As the populations of their home planets grew, population pressure forced most of the immortal Atlans to seek homes on uninhabited worlds. Eventually, like all the races of men when the cosmos was young, their own immortality forced them to seek homes elsewhere as they grew too big for even a good-sized world to support. So, as they increased in size and wisdom, they moved to more advanced worlds of the Elder Race, or else to larger, dark, uninhabited planets, there to stay until they became too large for even the larger planets—then a trek through space again in a few thousand years.

As vermin take over the homes of people when they have been deserted by the owners, so did the Jotun assume the discarded homes of the ever-migrating and growing Atlans and Titans. Worlds of outgrown and deserted mech were left by the continually growing races and it was this mech the Jotuns took as their own. Half the discoverable planets in this constellation are glutted with the ancient mech. Perhaps someday, the poor doomed men of this planet I hold so highly, my mother planet Mu, may find their way over the gulfs between the star-worlds and find this mech for their own betterment. Truly, the stores of these wondrous devices, bulging the labyrinthian caverns of thousands of planets are the "gifts" of the Gods. For the children that will follow us, we leave them—with our blessing.

Sometimes, however, there do appear dero races that, unluckily, escape the notice and supervision of the Elder Race, and they use for evil purposes the ancient mech of the Gods—mech designed and built for good, not evil. [15]

Such a race were the Jotuns—offsprings of what unknown evil life? Evil life walking upright in a parody of the dignity and good that is man, appropriating to their own evil uses the wondrous machines and mechanisms of the Gods, the Elder Race—the flying craft, the growth and nutrient mech, the healing ray devices, the awful, deadly war mech and other weapons from a dozen varying cultures of different states of progress.

There are times, in my voyages to strange, deserted worlds, when I wonder if the God Races were truly wise to leave, intact and complete, so much of their mech science that might be perverted to evil purposes by minds that have not the good in them that motivates the Elder Races. But then, the Elders have more knowledge and experience in such things than I—I am a mere twenty centuries grown. The Elders? Who really can say? Fifty Lemurian feet is my present height—and that took all those centuries. I have, on the Ruler Worlds of the Elders, seen some of the Gods that were easily three hundred or three hundred fifty Lemurian feet in height. They, alone, know how many centuries they have seen. Perhaps, though, even they could make an occasional mistake—a mistake like leaving equipment for the Jotun fleet heading toward us right now.

It was a motley array—the Jotun fleet. The black shape of Sathanas' space monster [16] rose in the background, ready to come in when the time and place looked inviting—poised for a crushing decisive blow.

We—the Aesir, Arl and I—had nothing to stop them with but the huge multi-ray I had devised. I radioed the Darkome to come in and back us up. The huge turntable creaked ponderously around on its improvised bearings taken from a dismantled elevator that was lifted from the depths. We turned it by the windlasses manned by the sweating warriors of the Aesir. It was no weapon for the swift flight of planes. Not at all. But, fortunately, the fliers were not trained for this sort of thing, and they missed most of their targets.

I had strict orders not to risk my life except in dire necessity. The Nor had no particular enthusiasm about wasting thousands of years of schooling in a moment's madness. And, here I was, drawn into this brawl of sun-mad dero without seeing any sort of way that I could honorably withdraw. I imagine Sathanas was cursing the risking of all his plans in the attack, too. He was mighty careful not to come within range of our huge multi-beam. The thunder of that distance splitter was deafening, its flames shot out for thirty miles in a coruscating ray of utter annihilation. I had no way of figuring its effective range, but it was a lot more than the thirty miles of its visible force. How to get into real action was the problem. It couldn't be done. But we kept them hopping, sweeping it up and down the whole line of battle. They couldn't bring up any heavy stuff at all. They couldn't blast us out of Asgard's walls—couldn't touch us except with an occasional bolt from the swooping fliers. Sathanas moved his ship up to what he calculated was the effective range of our big beam, and started blasting away with his power beams—big dissociators they were—and the walls dissolved in great clouds of rolling black smoke. Chunks fell, and he began to widen the breach.

I centered the big multi-beam on the Satana and played a card I had held back. Hoping to trap Sathanas into just this maneuver, I turned on the dissociator beam I had brought from the Darkome. Added to the other stuff the beam was made of, its effective range was immensely increased, for the multi-beam created a great path of ionization for it to travel over. The hull of the great ship, built of the most resistant materials manufactured by Nor, heated swiftly red and a gaping hole appeared in the black monster. Quick as thought, Sathanas blasted out of the range of our fumbling, snail-like beam. He did not take another chance with his ship.

It had been a close call, for him and for me, for I had little real knowledge of the strength or nature of the beams of which the great ray was composed. They were all obsolete forms of equipment of which I knew about theoretically, but in actual practical use I knew nothing. But the Atlans and Titans built such things well. They were as powerful and as uncorroded after two thousand years as they were the day they were built. Sometime I am going to spend a few years to learn everything there is to know about antique rays, both the actual equipment and the theoretical science behind their construction, for I will run into these hordes using the abandoned equipment again—if I am any ruler over my actions. I do not like their attitude toward war for war's sake, and I like the struggling bulldog idealism of such races as the Aesir. Handicapped by every evil—even their own thoughts play them false—they contrive to be good, jolly fellows, trustworthy, for the most part, and surprisingly able when emergency arises to call forth their best efforts.

As the Aesir began to acquire the knack of picking off the swooping fliers with their small rays, the whole battle dissolved into a great retreat of the Jotun forces to nurse their wounds and to prepare a real campaign. The range of the huge ray I had improvised from the odds and ends the Aesir had gathered together—work of centuries of life here—had saved the day for us.

"That will be all of that for a while," was Odin's comment, relieved at the easy victory over what had seemed vastly superior forces. We lost about a hundred men from the fire of the planes overhead, but, since a plane is a much bigger target than a man, the Jotuns paid several times over for this loss. There were a couple of thousand smoking holes in the walls and pavings from the fliers' rays and a two hundred foot breach in the walls. It did seem as though the Jotuns had decided the time was not ripe for a victory over the redoubtable Aesir whose reputation was greater than their prowess.

Odin continued, "They had no idea that we could reach them from here. They know little of the true uses of the old ray. That is certain. Sathanas has small stomach for real fighting, eh? I shall develop this use of many rays in one which you have shown me, and it will be a defense for Asgard for many years to come. Many lifetimes, maybe."

Odin's use of the word 'lifetimes' as a measurement of time struck me gloomily. Evidently the Aesir had lost all idea of fighting death, accepting it as an inevitable part of life. I shuddered to watch them down great drafts of water and ale, knowing that every drop of liquid on Earth contained some tiny particle of the dread radioactive material which is the cause of age. That a draught of water could become such a dread thing was a sad thought.

I resolved to do something about the future of the Aesir now. So, I said to Odin, "You Aesir are not an unworthy race. Long ago, on this very spot, there was a city called Atlansgard. Those people were the first colonizers to arrive here from the deeps of space and begin life when the Sun was young and clean. They were a mighty race, and they fought the primeval monsters of the world's youth, when growth had no end, and death did not confine size to a fixed measure for each species. That was the time of the Midgard serpent, who grew to nearly encircle the Earth, of Cronos who tried to eat all the life of Earth to keep his tremendous body in food. Those were the days of endless battle with the giants of growth whom hunger made mad, of the mad early Titans when the giants and men contended always for food and living space. Then government and the covenant came to Earth, to Mu, as men called the old planet then. Then came the time of real growth and goodness on earth, the Golden Age of Science when men pierced all mysteries with their minds. After a time, when the Sun began to age and bring age to Earth, the Atlans and Titans left Mu to dwell in dark space where no age is ever known. Now, you Aesir have grown here in Atlansgard and have taken the name of the great ancient Aesir to yourselves so that something of their greatness might adhere to your name. Well, you are not bad men, and I have a gift to offer you. Let me take with me into space a few of your young men with good heads on their shoulders. These I will teach the ways of navigation in deep space which is all that keeps your race from using the antique space ships which can still be found abandoned in the ancient caverns—abandoned because the Sun's radioactivity has infected the metal of their generators. Our law forbids such infected ships to be used by our races. But, you can use them to get away from the Sun, and I will train your men and send them back to you, and they can lead your people to a new home in space where the Sun is not an evil force. Then your race will remain forever young, instead of this pretense of immortality you now carry on for the benefit of your lessers. You would have the real thing—true immortality where there is no cause for age. What say you?"

Old Odin's eye shone—he had but one, though, the great ray he used was also called Odin's Eye—at the prospect of saving his race from age, and he knew enough of the ancient wisdom from the old writings to know I spoke the truth. There was my immense size, too, as a proof of unending, evergrowing youth to be found in the dark spaces. Too, the idea of finding the greater Elder Gods and learning true wisdom from them was to him the uttermost in attraction. He straightway selected three young Aesir. Vol, Vi and Zig were their names; for mentor and captain he sent the aging Tyr. I told the four to ready themselves, for I was starting back to my ship soon. I had long overstayed the allotted time for an immortal under an infectious sun's light.

As I talked to Odin, I was treated to a glimpse of what even comparatively ignorant men could do with the ancient science of magic, or 'mag-mech-ic,' as it was called in Atlan. The hundred or more corpses scattered about the walls of Asgard were gathered into a heap in the great hall of Gladsheim. Here, the Aesir's wise men and their maiden helpers concentrated beneficial rays from a dozen great generators upon the pile of dead. That transformation which has never lost its wonder for me took place. The hue of death faded from their cheeks; slowly they began to breathe. The wounds that bored through them—in some cases many times—began to close gradually, the Tagged red edges grew together as the healing of the ancient ben rays took place. When these slain warriors began to stir, the Aesir maidens picked them up and carried them to a place in the palace where smaller but more intense and potent ben rays were focused on their wounds to complete the healing process. The next day, most of them were again on their feet, nearly recovered. Yet, I knew that neither Odin nor his wise men had the slightest idea how to build or even repair the antique medical rays, nor had they even a proper curiosity about how its magic was accomplished. It was the "Ancient Gods' gift" was their attitude.

I realized that education was all this people needed to raise them to true God estate. But they needed such a lot of it. I cursed the fear that dwelt in the Great Ones of the dark spaces, forbidding them to come near any sun, even to rescue such men as these from the doom that already whitened the hair of many of them. Sometimes, I realized that even the High Gods have faults.

Well, I was one God who would lose that fault of too great fear of the hideous sun-death. I would find a way to rescue these Aesir.

I had assured Odin I would send the fleet of the Nor Space Patrol I expected to contact presently, to put the Jotuns in their place and to apprehend Sathanas. At the same time I radioed the Darkome to return to her former position on the Moon. Not enough time elapsed between the two messages for the Darkome to more than ready herself for flight. Why didn't I let the Darkome come on down in answer to my first message? She had ample fuel for several landings on planets no larger than Mu. I knew Sathanas was at hand, anxious to annihilate everyone such as myself who knew of his presence on Earth. Such is one's thoughts under infectious suns—always incorrect. It is a hard thing to remember always to do otherwise than what one's reason dictates when near a sun. I respect such races as the Aesir for this one reason—in spite of their life under the evil-making rays of the sun, they manage to remain good, reasonable fellows. Their bodies seem to build up a resistance to the mind distorting magnetic force of the sun, and they manage to think pretty clearly in spite of it. More power to that ability.

Everything was as beautiful as a powerful ben-ray illusion in a masterdream as we lifted in the tender toward the Moon. Tyr was thrilled as a warrior like him is thrilled by a battle-axe coming at his head, while the three young Aesir, Vol, Vi and Zig, their flashing teeth and glittering eyes told me that nothing had ever interested them so much as the sight of this little ship of mine. I wondered what would be their words when they saw for the first time the huge Dread-Nor Darkome lying in wait on the moon. Then it happened.

As the tender swiftly flashed upward toward the day-lit moon of early evening, the features of the shoreline and the city of Asgard blurred at our speed. In a matter of moments we were so high that the flat horizon of this green ball of Mu could be seen as the curve it is. I felt a glow of pride in my ship, my lovely Arl, and these four new-found friends. Like the sudden snap of a breaking glass perfume ball, our contentment was shattered.

"Mion!" gasped ever watchful Arl, "isn't that the Satana?"

"Awk! Why did that devil have to choose this time to take off?"

Arl, her face intense as a bird hypnotized by a snake, refused to take her eyes off the enemy craft.

"We're in a tight spot, Arl. If I change our course they can't fail to see us, and if I don't, we'll collide with them."

That's the way it was, too. Any change of speed or course would have been certain to attract their attention. I felt—and it was shortly proven true—that this was just one of those unhappy accidents that always seems to happen on a sun-cursed planet. The two ships hurtled upward to a junction.

At the last minute, I drove the tender hard over on the port side and down, hoping to dive past the Satana's stern and escape to the other side of the planet before they could come about. As our craft flashed past the enemy's starboard tail, the dread flash of tractor beams and dis (disintegration) rays reached over with clawing fingers for the shiny hull of my space boat. My hands were clammy with the tension of battle as I hit the lifter controls and desperately pulled the little craft up and down in short waves. Suddenly, we were dead astern of the Satana. For the moment they couldn't fire on us, but the game was discovered.

They must have known who we were. It was useless to hope for concealment. There was but one thing to do—and I did it.

I gave the brave little craft all the power she had, and ordering the rest to strap themselves in their seats, set her nose toward the surface of Mother Mu. We could feel the heat of the atmosphere being ground against our hull by the power of the little tender's drivers—powerful mechanisms that could drive the little boat between worlds if need be, but more power than was wise near the surface of a planet. And this violent maneuvering with a space ship so close to the surface wasn't wise either.

"Arl," I called, "where are they?"

"Oh, Mion, they have swung around—they're coming after us!"

Futilely I struck the driver lever, trying to coax just a bit more power from the gallant little machines—vibrating and smoking in their compartments. I knew they'd never last long being used like this.

"Now, Arl—what?"

"They're gaining, I think," sobbed Arl. "Mion, they're trying to reach us with their rays."

I swung the craft to the right and then frantically to the left—all the while diving in a long, flat curve toward Earth—

Bang!

With a bone jarring wrench, one of the enemy's tractor beams wrapped tenuous fingers around the little tender's hull, then locked tight. From full speed, we were quickly slowed and drawn toward the Satana. A horrible, painful sensation—tractor beams lock on every atom of the object they hold—like being clawed inside.

We were lost.

The enemy drew his prey swiftly to the air-lock that surrounded the tractor-beam turret holding us and pulled us inside.

With a jar they set the tender on the floor of the airlock. We couldn't move. The crew of the enemy craft swarmed into the air-lock after closing the outer port.

As they scrambled over the tender toward the entrance hatch, I took a look at Arl's strained features and refused to think—probably the last good look I would take at that lovely face.

Footnotes

15 GOD-BUILT MECH: In the ancient world wide caverns that some old, old race built and then deserted. they had many marvelous mechanisms. When they left this planet, Mother Mu or Lemuria (See previous issues of Amazing Stories), the deadly rays that were emanating from the Sun had infected their machines and mechanisms, and so, to protect themselves from the death that they contained, the Elder Race left ALL of their tools of life—everything—behind them and then departed to far, friendly, star-homes where they live on even today. But as they live they grow, like the Giant Redwood trees of our own California, and by now, this ancient race is too big to tread the paths of Earth.

Their stimulating machines were designed for pleasure and their growth science was meant to assist Nature—but that is not the use they get today. The degenerate humans that live in the caves pervert the antique mech to evil uses, and the machines, being infected with sun poison, make the evil users more evil—a vicious circle that is almost impossible to stop for several reasons. First, surface men doubt the existence of these things, and, secondly, their mech makes them infinitely more potent and powerful than surface men.—R. S. Shaver.

16 SATHANAS' SPACE MONSTER: These untellably ancient space ships are huge beyond belief ... as large as the rigid, lighter-than-air Zeppelins of Earth were before the war—the Los Angeles, the Akron, the Hindenburg, etc. They were small craft compared to the antique spacers. For instance, dirigibles 800 to 1000 feet long with a diameter 80 to 120 feet would not offer much room or comfort for a man 50 to 60 feet tall, particularly on long space flights. Then, too, that size wouldn't offer much room for the necessary space equipment—drivers, stores, motors, etc.

Dirigibles are the largest flying machines modern man has made, yet, large as they are, they are comparable in size merely to the tender of the big Nor craft in the story, the Darkome.

For possible accounts of these space ships being seen in recent times, see Charles Fort's books.

On October 23, 1822, two unknown, dark bodies crossing the sun were observed by Pastorff (Am. Sci. Disc., 1860-411).

Seven months later, May 22, 1823, an unknown shiny thing was seen near the planet Venus by the astronomer Webb (NATURE, 14195).

There is no basis for assuming that these unknown objects were satellites. They would have to be very large even to be thought of as moons.

Furthermore, Charles Fort quotes from the ANNALES DE CHIMIE, 30-417—"objects that were seen by many persons, in the streets of Embrun, during the eclipse of Sept. 7, 1820, moving in straight line, turning and retracing in the same straight lines, all of them separated by uniform spaces."

Two unknown dark bodies crossing the sun, a shiny thing near Venus, and objects moving in geometric patterns in this same general area, and all reported within a matter of months of each other—all these things seem to indicate unknown SHIPS or something—OF HUGE, ALMOST PLANETOID SIZE moving under intelligent control.

Were these actually spacers of the Elder Race? Men see only what they want—or are supposed to see.

Some idea of the size of the artificial caverns built by the Elder Race beneath the surface of this Earth can be gained when one recalls that the tender and Sathanas' ship both flew into the shafts and caverns. It was in the caverns that they were manufactured, and it was there that they were stored. The sight of one of these incredibly ancient cave hangars with several ancient spacers abandoned over the floor is breathtaking in its immensity, and unbelievable, in fact.—Author.

CHAPTER VI.

IN THE HANDS OF SATHANAS

Sathanas' family was one of the few families of variforms among the Nor. Accepted as exiles long ago from some variform city of the Angles of Earth, the Satanic family was a clovenfooted one, something like Arl in general makeup, but with shaggy black hair on their legs and of a very dark complexion, with horns showing Titan blood somewhere in the family tree.

We were taken directly to his chambers. His dark form loomed ahead of us in the red mist of his nutrient air—of his own formula, and probably one of the causes of his evil character, for it had a smell like nothing I had ever experienced before. Some chemical he had added to the usual formula had fooled him into thinking it was beneficial, but was more than likely a dangerous stimulant and had weakened his body's insulative resistance to detrimental flows of energy. His character had certainly become that of a mad deco of the most dangerous kind, for his wisdom, untempered with concern for any other life, would be a never-ending horror to all men unless he were stopped. It didn't look as if Mutan Mion would be able to do much about stopping Sathanas.

A pretty predicament for the reputation of Mutan Mion. When my comrades would come to hear how I had fallen into the hands of Sathanas without a blow being struck, there would be many a head shaken behind my back. Sad, sad shakes of Nortan heads. Murmurs of "Tch, tchtoo bad. Mion might have been such a noble specimen but—the Sun infection, you know." And the others would nod silently in agreement and touch their foreheads with their finger-tips. Then, despite all the god-like qualities that they did possess, they would feel very smug and complacent. They would make a sincere attempt within their minds to—well, not forgive exactly, but—explain what the cause of my trouble was, and they would sympathize patronizingly. They'd think, "His unfortunate Earth background and birth; he lacks real stamina—resource—too bad." I always had to contend with that in my work among the God-men of Nor—they worried about the evil that had roamed on Earth expelling the Titans and Atlans and some foolish ones thought that everyone of Earth might—no, must—be affected.

Not all the men of Nor thought thusly, however. Most of that great race of Elders peered deeply into problems and didn't overlook any facts in arriving at the right answers. But I have found in all races and peoples in the planets I have trod that there are those who pass judgment on half facts. Fortunately for the progress on intelligence, those foolish ones are not too many among the Elder Races.

Sathanas, though infected by a taint of the deadly "de" from the Sun, usually collected facts—all of them—before making any of his illegal moves. The one error he'd made had caused me to chase him here to Mu, but I had been the one to err when we'd come too close to the deadly, treacherous Sun, and I was in his toils.

My lovely Arl and I and those valiant young Aesir were taken prisoners, they who had so blindly put their lives into my hands—lives that were not immortal as the lives of we of the Elder Races, 'tis true, but lives that were, nevertheless, well thought of by their owners. All those lives had been entrusted to me—to their belief in my legendary ability to carry success with me. And what had I done? I had fallen into as stupid error as any inhabitant of the Sun's planets. What was worse for one of my almost god-like status, I had been trapped like a green cadet on his first solo space patrol—trapped without firing a shot, without the semblance of a struggle. Trapped and taken. There was nothing to be done about it now but to take as stoically as we could whatever foul torments our captor could devise.

It is not often that a proud member of the Elder Races stands captive before a creature such as this Sathanas.

The tender had been forced open in the air-lock of the Satana, and the evil crew of that black craft had ordered us out of it with little ceremony. At this close range, there was no point to attempt to overpower the crew, right in the very bowels of the enemy ship, so we allowed ourselves to be escorted into the presence of the Satana's master.

Sathanas sat surrounded by his women, his dark face gloating evilly. As we were led before him, we could hear his ill-repressed sigh of satisfaction at the prize his luck had won for him.

The first time I saw him I found him distasteful, and I had no more enthusiasm for him now. I thought that because we were of the Elder Races we weren't to fare too badly at his hands, and again I erred. Perhaps the Sun was beginning to affect me.

Slowly I glanced around the chamber—his own personal quarters judging by the wealth and luxury that had been expended on it. I have said that he was surrounded by women? That makes it sound like just a few—but there seemed to be scores of women here. And almost as many planetary races as there were women. His agents and slave raiders had done their job well. The place was full of women and girls culled—literally hand picked—from the beauties of a hundred far flung planet cities. From the looks of things, Sathanas had first choice of all the women his agents acquired for all of his illegal pleasure palaces that flourished in spite of all the laws of the Gods.

Now there are some pleasure palaces run by wise men, and very good things they are too, but some are only "apparently" good, concealing hideous evil behind a perfect facade of beneficence. These were served by men (or creatures that walk like men) like Sathanas—surface good concealing abysmal and horrible depravity.

All these beautiful women surrounding Sathanas were the end products of the hidden vices of the immortal Elder Races—vices that were unsuspected for a long time. True, these vice-ridden Elders were not very numerous, but, like every other race in Time, there are always some who do not measure up to the standard of the tribe—whether their lack is known or not. Perhaps certain ones have physical afflictions, and others, mental, but there always seems to be that little group that is incomplete or evil or decadent. Such was a certain element amongst the Elder Races—good and noble on the surface, but their minds were evil—or inclined to evil.

Where there is a profit to be made from evil that men do or desire, there will be other men to act to gratify evil desires and line their pockets. That was what Sathanas was—a panderer possessing immortality and catering to a mass of immortal degenerates—to their lusts and cruelty, procuring for their lusts, women and girls and for their cruelty, men, women and children of a hundred different races and colors. Their cruelty demanded unconditioned victims, but their lusts required refinements—refinements that no one knows for how many years have been improved and intensified.

These women around Sathanas, and I don't know how many thousands of others, had been made into something that was part human and part pure horror—made into robot servants of vast and synthetic forces beyond their poor strength to fight in any way—made by forces that can, and do, mould and pervert even the best natured person into something that is not human—into a tool or instrument of pleasure, or an instrument of torture of the most insidious kind. Robot women whose minds the Elder mechanisms had perfected in some ways to beauty while other parts of their minds had been destroyed.

Centuries of the control of stimulation rays had caused their thought processes to be—not thoughts of the normal human. Rather, they were merely mental reaction to outside stimulation. They served others' purposes with the products of their minds as well as the motions of their bodies. The shape of their lips, the seductive sleekness of their bodies, the looks of longing and desire in their eyes. [17]

Footnotes

17 SIRENS: The authors are of the opinion that the alterations done upon the slave women of the Nor vice rings, carried on less efficiently here on Earth in the past, may be the factual origin of worldwide legends of sirens and goddesses of love as differentiated from female deities supposed to oversee fertility and procreation.

In the Hellenic Pantheon, Diana is usually imagined as the goddess of Fertility and Aphrodite, the goddess of Love. Thus, here we have the case where Aphrodite COULD have been an outstanding creation of some of the vice ring or perhaps merely one of those latter day, almost-immortal humans that, in legend, became the lesser Gods and Goddesses.

In the legend of Ulysees, he had himself tied to the mast of his ship, after sealing the ears of his crew with wax, so that none of them could be beguiled by the enchanting voices of the sirens living on the treacherous, rock-bound shores. (In the story, certain female slaves were trained in various arts, much as the Geisha of Japan—specialists in various branches of entertainment.) Quite naturally, that would include girls that sang, and suppose that some of them were to escape? And, need we point out that these legends of sirens are almost world wide, but notably in Greece and in the Teutonic legends? Girls whose ("RAY-altered) voices were so compelling that even so primary an urge as self-preservation was thrown overboard in the victim's attempt to get closer to these infinitely desirable voices.—Author.

CHAPTER VII.

A VALUABLE CHUNK OF MEAT

The awe-struck Aesir with me didn't guess that the voluptuous, desirable women around Sathanas were poor mindless creatures; machine-made to appeal to base masculine senses of some members of the immortal Elder Races. They didn't know that what they gazed upon was false and inhuman. They knew only that they saw here women beautiful and desirable beyond their wildest dreams—the fevered dreams of the Earthmen that they were. Here were dream creatures smiling at them through half-lidded eyes ... sending their blood racing. And mirroring the gaze of Sathanas' women, the eyes of the young Aesir were pinwheels of hungry fire.

Although it takes several moments to tell, I knew instantly what these women were—and a quick look at my new friend from fair Mu confirmed the fact that the agents and mech controllers of Sathanas had done their work well—the Aesir had lost their senses to the lure of the devil's women.

I looked at Arl. She, too, knew what lay behind all this unholy scenery and her little nose was raised, proudly disdainful. Her eyes stared past Sathanas and all the false finery around him.

"My lovely Arl is just going to ignore all this. Good girl!" I chuckled to myself. But the chuckle died in my throat as I came to a halt in front of Sathanas—the hidden, deadly evil, ill-concealed in those smoky eyes didn't promise much of enjoyment for us captives standing before him.

He glanced up from the snowy throat he'd been kissing, and our eyes locked. At first, there was just that evil stare. Then . . . recognition! With that, he became alive and casually tossed the attentive female from his lap, as a normal man would dispose of a puppy when other business called. With a displeased frown the poor creature glared at me for interrupting her pleasure, but she scurried to one side, followed by the hungry eyes of the Aesir, for she was about the same size as they. Evidently she was a new acquisition. After dismissing her, Sathanas had placed both hands on the arms of his "stim" chair and looked at us from under his dark brows.

Finally the dog deigned to speak.

"Ah, my dear Mutan Mion," the words were like the treacherous hiss of a deadly snake, and the smile that went with it was equally reptilian. "Ah, yes, and his lovely wife, the beautiful Arl."

When he mentioned her name, I would have strangled him had I been free to move . . . his using her name was profane. He had bowed as he spoke it.

"You know, Fair Lady, the tales that are told do not do justice to the beauty that you do have. I am honored by this visit from such a famous pair. I have many times read the record of your progress in the past centuries. I am grieved that I must welcome you in such poor surroundings as my little craft provides."

I said nothing. In fact, I tried desperately not to think of anything that his thought-readers might find of value.

"Oh, come, Mion, surely you haven't lost that oratorical tongue that we have heard of so much? Can't you speak?"

"The less I say, the better, O mighty Sathanas. I am not numbered among your admirers."

At that he frowned. There was no use to hide the truth or crawl to his ego. I knew that a dozen telaugs were playing over us and certainly some of them transferred our thoughts to him. I didn't care for him or any of his kind.

Sathanas had looked like he was going to lose his temper, but he recovered his front of suavity. Just as he was ready to speak again, he was interrupted.

The Aesir, Tyr, was more accustomed to lacing such characters than I and he had immediately adopted the best possible attitude for the moment.

"Your majesty!" said Tyr, "the Arch-Angel of the heavens, the one mighty man of blood and war that I have always wanted to meet! Oh! Mighty One, that black flag of yours is the banner and desire of every warrior who reiishes true freedom!"

Even with the information that his "spy" rays were undoubtedly sending him, this spontaneous flattery from Tyr caught Sathanas momentarily off his guard, and he frowned darkly . . . puzzled.

"Why the gloomy frown?" asked Tyr. "Is the mighty Sathanas displeased at the offer of service from such fighters as these?" Tyr indicated the others. "Why only today, My Lord, we put the mighty Jotun to flight outside our city of Asgard . . . what better recommendation could a warrior bring you?"

Tyr was doing a valiant job of bluffing, but he couldn't know that the only "war" that Sathanas ever had any contact with was drunken space-men's brawls, or violent kidnapings and perhaps in arranging the monetary details of warfare on some of the other "der" planets. The Aesir tried, but his bluff failed.

At the mention of the battle outside the walls of Asgard, Sathanas blackened and shot to his feet. Some trinket or other that he had in his hand went violently to the floor.

"So! . . . so!" The huge fiend was raging but not saying much. I could see his lips quivering with self-indulgent anger. "So! It was you, Mion, who pierced the hull of my best and newest battle ship! You . . . you are the upstart who is poking his nose into my affairs here in my refuge!"

He had bunched his fist and stood shaking it under my nose while I stood still, not moving a muscle.

"You insolent . . . you uncultured freak. It will not be you that carries the tale of my doings back to Nor! You can take the word of the Lord Sathanas for that!"

The miserable cur emphasized his last remark with a slap on the face that would have earned him death had I not been held in the grip of a watching control-ray. I kept silent. There was nothing for me to say. Sathanas ranted on.

"Centuries ago, you came to the Council Chambers on Nor and received more honors and recognition than all my labors have ever brought me. You rose steadily in power in the so-called government of Nor. And, as the final insult, you approach, no, you even eclipse the power of men three times your age!"

He was being carried away by his own thwarted ambitions. The more he raved, the more he became flecked with foam, like a stallion raced too hard. He was stomping back and forth in front of us. Every eye in the room was watching him, and it was only our little group that wasn't cowering at the sight and sound of his anger.

"But, my dear MUTAN MION! Your . . . luck . . . has . . . ended! You are in my power now—I, who am now the open enemy of all the base servants of the Nor Empire, and I will see that you die . . . slowly, painfully!" He threw back his head and laughed like a man gone mad. "Haw! and those so dainty hounds of our so high God-head—that thrice cursed Nor Patrol—will receive the complete sensation record of your death, with my compliments!"

That must have pleased him for he calmed down and smiled. "Ah ha, THAT should keep them somewhat less hot on my trail, knowing the painful fate of the great Mu-tan Mion who unluckily caught up with me. Me . . . Sathanas!"

And he didn't mean to miss any nuance of sadistic pleasure. He pranced over to where Arl was standing, his black cloven hooves making the only sound in the room. She still was staring past him as he stroked the little black beard he affected.

His fevered eyes gazed up and down the glorious body of my beloved Arl and I swore to myself that if I were ever free I would tear those insulting eyes out with my own bare hands.

"Beautiful!" He nodded. "Mion, your Arl is a very valuable looking chunk of meat [18].

At least, she will be valuable when my colleagues get finished with a few slight mental operations on her. No doubt you are familiar with the slight adjustments that we make on these lovely women's minds to enhance their value? No? That's a pity. And she is big, too. I'm sure there are some among the Nor men that will pay a pretty price to have such a sturdy plaything to take with them to the heavy planets. Perhaps I shall keep her here for my own use . . . for a little while, anyway. And, then, maybe I can reward one of the Jotun chiefs with her for certain favors that they have done me in the past.

Mustering his courage, he reached up, and stripped Arl of the few garments that she wore, the better to inspect his new property.

"They say that Mion's Arl is one of the most expert manipulators of the 'stim' machines. Mmmm, I believe I know where such a woman of her size and ability with 'stim' would bring a fortune, and the size of a Ruler's ransom, too."

Evidently he was tired of merely taunting his captives without them saying anything, for he suddenly ordered, "Take them away!"

Obeying his command, the heavy ray that had held us captive was released and some of the ship's crew with small hand rays shackled us with them.

They didn't have them turned up to full power—they couldn't have, because all I could feel was a slight drag. As soon as I realized what was up—that I was free—I raced for the throat of the fiend now returning to his couch, hurling his sycophants and dancing girls to the right and left like a farmer sowing grain. Just as my fingers were about to clench about his neck, a beam from one of the ever watchful servitors struck me down at his feet, a contorted bundle of agony. The epilepto-ray [19] that they used was the most painful known to Nor science—forbidden except for experimental laboratory work to discover a counter for it.

I rolled in tortured convulsions on the floor. Just as my last grip on consciousness slipped from my grasp, I saw my lady Arl folding like a wounded bird and something that she had tried to use as a weapon fell from her grasp . . . or was that blood!

Footnotes

18 MEAT: Cannibalisim has been practiced for centuries in the now almost sterile caverns—dero eating tero, perhaps tero eating dero; both, it is suspected, capturing by means of the ancient "mech" (mechanism) surface people for food. They consider surface people merely a higher species of food-animal. Throughout the caverns, we of the surface are referred to, not as "surface" people, but "meat" people.

   No doubt the European dero ate heartily beneath the concentration camps. We suspect that it was they who activated the Nazis guarding the camps to the abysmal depths of depravity to which they descended. For centuries, the dero have been doing the same things—and worse—though on a smaller scale.

   The Jotuns were, no doubt, dealers in "meat" delicacies.—R. S. Shaver.

19 EPILEPTO RAYS: The epilepto ray was originally intended for the use of the Elder Race's Police. By means of it, primitive tribes, wild animals, and even rioting or uncontrollable members of the race itself could be brought under control, harmlessly. However, as with all the ancient mechanisms, the Elder scientists continually improved them, and at times these improvements called for regulation by the Ruling Council to limit their use to insure the general safety of the entire race.

   Some of the epilepto ray projectors are still extant in the caverns here an Earth, and their use by the dero (degenerate humans) cause torment and paralysis to a lot of the surface people.

   The ray itself, in action, contorts every muscle of the victim's body by means of an alternating current of synthetic pain-ray electric, the pulsations resulting in that spasmodic jerking so apparent in one suffering a so-called "epileptic" fit.—Author.

CHAPTER VIII.

UNDER THE PAIN RAY

"Oooooh, Mi . . . Mion . . ."

Hearing these moans and my name through a fuzzy humming in my ears, I tried to open my eyes and raise myself up. I couldn't. Then, gradually, with the return of consciousness, I realized that I was aching to the ends of my feet. I opened my eyes.

Above my head was the cause of that aching I felt. Now that I was awake and conscious, it wasn't just an ache, it was pain. There above my head was a slowly swinging pendulum, the end of which held a vari-pain ray lens and it was this sweeping motion of the ray that made me feel pain all over my body. I couldn't move from under it. I tried, but the crew of the Satana had too much practice with binding captives in chains for me to do more than tighten a few of the more uncomfortable ones around my wrist and ankles. I could move my head, and turning around I saw whence came the moans and my name. The brave Aesir were chained down alongside me. That was fiendish—chaining Earthmen in range of a pain ray that was nearly killing a fifty foot immortal member of the Elder Races [20].

They were moaning softly and I felt the tears come to my eyes with pride in these men that old Mother Mu could still produce. Men suffering agonizing torture and just barely moaning—the same as a young boy of, say, ten years being tortured on a crude Jotun rack without making a sound. They must be near crazy with the torment. I was myself. Sathanas, it seemed, did not intend to have his guests miss any of the dubious comforts that he could provide.

I figured that we must be some place in the lower hold of the Satana—no ports were visible, just the blank dull metal walls. There was something missing, though I couldn't decide exactly what.

ARL!

"Arl! Arl . . . where are you?" I called, thinking that perhaps she might be in the same cell as we, but placed so that I couldn't see her. That hope was destroyed when Tyr, sobbing with the pain he was suffering, said, "My Lord . . . ugh . . . they didn't bring her with us . . ."

"Tyr, what did they do with her?" My concern for Arl made me forget for a moment the awful torment, the horrible spasms of pain that dropped like blood from our bodies.

". . . I don't know . . . Lord Mion! Are we dying? This . . . pain . . . I can't stand it!"

"Easy, friend Tyr," I tried to comfort him, "they will not keep this up until we die . . . they're too cruel for even that. This is just a sample of what we are in for. Courage, friends."

My beloved Arl . . what had these accursed fiends done to her? How long had I lain in this cell unconscious? Sathanas had admitted some of the foul things he planned for my wife. Had he had time to carry out some of them?

I strained at the chains; I had to get free. I failed. And these poor Aesir warriors were near death with pain. Something had to be done. But what?

I had it. Hypnosis!

These men were of a lower mental calibre than myself, understandable when you realized that I had twenty centuries to develop while they had barely that many years. Hypnosis would serve two purposes—take their minds off the pain they were enduring and fill them with subconscious information that we might be able to use if the scales of Fortune fell in our direction.

I commenced to talk to them, soothing their pain as much as I could with my voice. It wasn't long until they were in that stage half way between total hypnosis and consciousness. That was the best I could do, considering that we were operating under extreme difficulties, being bound and continually swept with the vari-pain beam. From talking about them and their families to fix their interest, I had gradually worked the talk around to technical subjects. I wanted to teach them as much of spacemanship as I could under the circumstances.

"At the mid-space-point between two attracting spatial bodies," I explained, beginning with the most elementary principles of interstellar astrogation, "lies a thin 'zone of neutralization'—a thin zone where all matter is weightless."

"We have heard you mention that before, Lord Mion," spoke one of the Aesir from his bed of artificial pain.

"Well, friends, that 'zone of neutralization' is important. It is the knowledge and the use of the peculiarities of the way all mass is inertially neutralized there that enables us to journey between the farthest stars."

"Why is that, Mion?"

"Because, starting a star trip anywhere else would be impossible. There would be too much mass to overcome. It would be impossible to achieve the needed acceleration quick enough."

The Aesir were doing their best to follow what I was telling them—but now they could only groan.

"It's like ... like ... the difference between jumping off the top branch of a bushy tree and jumping off a wall. In the one, drag at the start slows you down somewhat, whereas, in going off the wall, there is nothing to slow your acceleration. Do you see, friends?"

"Aye, Lord, we hear .." They struggled to suppress the shrieks that hammered at their lips for voice.

"Now, Warriors, listen carefully. It is there, in the 'zone of complete lack of weight' that all long, interstellar flights MUST begin ... always remember to be very careful in pointing your ship on the exact course to your distant objective lest your course intersects another path where some object may lie that would destroy you in the event of a collision."

When they had indicated that they understood that, I continued.

"Poised motionless in the exact center of the 'zone,' and pointing in the correct direction, the ship is given full power of all the plates [21] at once. Ordinarily, such instant application of all the power at rest would kill all the ship's passengers, but at the EXACT center of the 'zone' ANY acceleration can be achieved without danger, depending upon the amount of power impetus."

Again they groaned acceptance of what I had said.

"When you give your ship full throttle as I've told you, it will instantly attain vast velocity depending on the power of your ship's plates and how carefully you balanced your ship in the center of the 'zone'. Keep applying power, and in a short time you will find yourself far beyond your starting point. Like a flash you will be in the region of the stars which are unfamiliar to you, traveling at a speed your Earth brains cannot comprehend. If you were watching a spacer accelerate from the 'zone', it would seem to you that the ship had vanished. No motion would be seen. It would be there one moment and disappear the next—disappear into nothingness. Such is the speed of ships that fly between the stars. Using this tremendous speed, you can fling yourself far beyond the light of this deadly, evil Sun and within the regions of space that the Elder Races, the Gods of the Aesir, have chosen as their dwelling place."

"Would not we humans be in danger from the wrath of our Gods for daring to come to them, Lord Mion?"

"No, my friends, once in the general area of the dark planets, you would soon be overtaken by some space patrol and, your intentions being understood, you would be helped in every way to find yourselves a home far from the deadly 'de', a home near those of the Gods. Have you understood?

All four of the Aesir groaned their answer: "Aye, Lord Mion, we have understood . . . you . . . and will do as . . . you advise . . . if . . . there ever comes ... the time when we are ... free of the clutches of this Sathanas."

There were other things I explained to the Aesir, things like how the first light speed is achieved with a light impetus but as the interstellar space ships move into as much as fifty-speeds, the 'ether drag' increases on the order of one unit of drag to fifty units of light speed.

Thus, the required impetus needed to achieve one light speed is increased by one for each additional fifty light speeds. Actually, no body in the known cosmos is ever entirely weightless, but there are conditions where a given mass or body loses apparent weight to the point where its weight is negligible. The best place to achieve this condition of weightlessness is that area that I've told you about ... the area between the world or other spatial bodies that we term the "zone of weightlessness."

I went on and on with my talking and explaining, more to keep from thinking than from any hope of teaching these long suffering friends over-much. The pain, or rather, the perception of the pain, had gradually increased almost to the point of madness for the victim. No doubt the fiends that served Sathanas were making a thought record of all our sensations and words as the master of this depraved vessel had promised to send to my friends in the Nor Patrol.

"Course must be plotted and ship poised exactly in the center of the zone..."

"... hit such zones every time you pass between worlds ... maintain acceleration..."

The pain never stopped ... on and on ... pain ... waves of agony ... some smooth strokes of torment ...

"Use the devices that the builders have installed to determine the center ... full throttle ... trust instruments..."

Flashes of memory came and went in the delirium of our fevered agony ... what I said ... gone ...

The young Aesir had good minds though very little real education. I could not have taught them any mathematics, even had my hands been free to do so. It would be fortunate, indeed, if they remembered any of the facts of space navigation that I was trying to get across to them. I, myself, am not certain of all that I told them. The longer we were chained under the vari-pain ray, the more our minds slipped from our conscious control. A living body can stand only so much of nerve vibration.

This torment had been going on for hours ... painful ... moments of release when it reached the ends of its swings and then that laving with agony again.

It may have been days ... or weeks ... I don't know ... just back and forth ... pain.

Footnotes

20 SIZE OF THE ELDER RACE: The authors suggest that anyone interested get a copy of Charles Fort's "Lo!" In Chapter Nine. he .discusses the findings, BY PRESENT DAY HUMANS, of the skeletons of huge creatures 40 to 65 feet in length. The conventional "scientific" explanation is that they are the skeletal remains of whales washed up on the shore. Fort refutes this sort of illogic by pointing out that whales' skeletons do not have BROAD HIP BONES.

He also mentions a report from the LONDON DAILY NEWS. In it is recounted the dredging up of a large skull from the north of Scotland, of a size that the authorities claimed would fit an elephant, but it would have to have been a large one to boast eye-sockets a foot across. We suggest, for those interested in such research, that it MIGHT have been the skull, preserved somehow (or, perhaps, fairly recently dispatched), but a skull, nevertheless, of one of the ancient Giants that built the caves beneath our world. (Excerpt is from the Daily News, June 6, 1908.)

If the eyes are a gauge of the full size of the completed skeleton, the creature (a member of the Elder Race?) would have to have been at least 40 feet tall.—Author.

21 DRIVER PLATES: In the two thousand years since Mutan's visit to Earth, the ships used by him have developed and adopted the drive plate instead of the gas jet drive. Both are rocket drives in principle, but different in detail. The drive is an alloy metal that decomposes into a repellant electric flow very

much like gravity in reverse. Things fall away from the plate when certain frequencies of dis-electric are applied to the plate. The resultant impulse is rendered useful by a reflecting material, opaque to the drive flow, on the side of the plate nearest the ship. Hence all the repellant flow is directed backward—giving a drive like a rocket in principle but very different in detail. This is the drive generally used in the ancient ships—though there are several distinct types of drives—and ships from widely separated civilizations lying about the caverns, still today existant, and in some cases still usable.—Author.

CHAPTER IX.

SEIZING THE SATANA

As one will, under the 'der' influence of a sun that burns heavy metals and makes men's minds function in evil error, I had spent my time waiting for—what? Some silly pap to my vanity—a feather in my cap that would be mine had I captured this fellow Sathanas single-handed. And what had the 'der' sun led me to? Capture—and worse, torture for myself and my four valiant companions . . . and . . . the Gods of Space only know what horrible fate for my lovely Arl. True, I had some idea that Sathanas was not going to kill me—that would have been too merciful for his evil dero soul. No, he meant to prolong my torment to its last groan, preferably, hoping that it would take years for me to groan my last.

"That was small consolation, knowing that he wasn't going to kill me. But, a human body can stand only so much. My companions had fainted long ago. I must have fainted several times myself. I was aware of several periods of consciousness. Perhaps that fiend was merely reviving me in order to see my huge frame collapse again in an effeminate faint that would have given him great pleasure, no doubt.

But, as I say, I revived the last time. And, from somewhere within me came rage—rage that lent my tortured body strength . . . strength that Vanue's marvelous nutrients [22] had given me, over and above my natural inheritance.

Had Sathanas known all that Vanue knew about nutrient and beneficial rays, he probably would not have become what he was, but instead he would have grown into a wise and noble man. As it was, his men had failed fully to realize the tremendous power that had been grown into my limbs. I didn't know it myself until that final moment when my agonized body could take no more and with supreme rage and pain, a mighty roar issued from my straining throat and I heaved on the chains that held me strapped to the floor—heaved until I could feel the warm blood from my lacerated wrists.

There was a sight—a mighty fifty-foot God-man flat on his back, his head thrown hard against the floor, his back arched with the massive, bowed muscles that quivered with the last supreme, flayed effort for a futile final flail against its bonds. Suddenly, my cry of rage turned to one of joy—sheer animal joy. One of the chains had pulled loose from the moorings in the floor! A catlike smile lighted my face as I grasped the chain on my other arm and pulled with savage joy on that mere chain with both my massive arms. It came free!

With both arms unchained, it was the work of a moment to loose myself of the chains binding my feet and I stood up. Free! Free, for the first time in hours . . . or was it days? Released from my bonds, but not entirely free as I learned after a moment's thought. I still had to get out of this cell—but I was standing, and on my feet. I could fight now.

I stepped from under the vari-pain beam, and, at once, I disposed of that with one vicious swipe of my balled fist. Then, 1 set about freeing my unconscious companions. That was done in a moment.

The five of us were released from our bonds. The only thing between us and complete freedom was a metal door and the crew of this war vessel of Sathanas' fleet, perhaps some three or four hundred men of the approximate size of myself. Quite a formidable obstacle under normal circumstances, but, just out of my bonds as I was, it didn't seem unconquerable. There was something in being able to move one's limbs that make other difficulties seem of less importance and of no consequence.

After making certain that my four Aesir were still living and would soon snap out of their stupor, I tried the metal door. It seemed strong enough. Then I really put my strength to the handle and with an oath to the unknown gods of spacemen, I braced my legs against the wall and pulled. The sweat stood out on my brow, my muscles ached with the tremendous load, the calves of my legs were quivering with the awful strain—then, with a shriek of tortured metal, the lock tore out and the door flew open, flinging me to the floor with the sudden reaction. I sprawled on the deck, a very much surprised and bruised God.

When breath finally came back to me, I mumbled something about "Our friend Sathanas must have been too unwise in some of his remarks to our Nortan engineers for such a weak bit of equipment to be installed in a warship . . . ha! Serves him right!"

It was true. There are no finer craftsmen anywhere in all the known cosmos, yet they are sometimes prone to strike back, thusly, for some slight insult—letting inferior work pass as O.K. Then, one day, the one that insulted will find his mech failing when he needs it most. It pays to be courteous and considerate with everyone, I have found in twenty centuries of ruling. It pays.

Where this monster ship was heading, I had no idea. I did have the idea that I didn't wish to go wherever it was going—it no doubt wouldn't have been healthy.

My reverie was interrupted by a moan. I looked to the Aesir who were beginning to stir themselves. Tyr was the first to come to, and with his help we soon had the other three on their feet and spoiling for a fight, We all wanted vengeance for that period under the vari-pain machine, and we meant to get it.

Out the door I went, the four Aesir stalking behind me, an eager light in their eyes and a look of supreme faith in my judgment and ability on their faces.

We rounded a curve in the companionway and nearly barged into a ray-post unannounced. At the controls of the huge space gun sat a big

Angle in the uniform of Sathanas' service, on watch for some sign of the Nor Patrol.

"Let's take 'im!" I yelled, bounding forward at the same time, seizing the man's arms and twisting them back and up. The Aesir needed no second urging. They swarmed over the huge fellow, one of them standing on his lap and stuffing part of his coat in the Angle's mouth to smother any outcry.

"Get his weapons, Tyr!" I ordered.

Tyr was tugging at the warrior's weapon belt and it came free. I couldn't help laughing, even in so crucial a moment, at the startled look on the fellow's face. Evidently he had never expected this. The fellow's dis gun Tyr gave to Vol, then he pulled out his flame sword and finding it too big, asked if I wanted it. I shook my head, "No, Tyr, it too small for me." He flung it aside.

"Come with me, my evil friend," I said to the fellow whose arms must have been hurting him for the way I had them twisted behind him. With my invitation, I pulled the big guy to his feet and propelled him along in front of me down the corridor.

Adjacent to the cargo compartment where we had lain I had noticed another empty cell. I hurled our captive into it and locked the door.

Vi, one of the Aesir, shot a penetrative ray through the door and we could see the big one struggling to his feet. "Give him the epilepto-ray, Vi," I ordered.

Flicking a little lever on the barrel of the gun he held, the ray changed color slightly and we could see the poor dupe in the cell fall, writhing in pain, to the floor. Well, we had had a lot worse at their hands. When he stopped moving, we knew he was paralyzed for the next few hours.

I began to like these Aesir more and more. There is something in the way a fighting man operates that gladdens the heart of another warrior, and these Aesir had jumped to action with alacrity that would have done credit to the noblest of the Nor. And Tyr was the best of the four. There is nothing that can replace experience in battle, and they all had that and more. Tyr, though, was a companion that I would find myself reluctant to give up . . . quiet, but quick . . . reflective and slow of speech, but fast as a snake when necessity called. There are few like him, yet, according to the Nor medicoes, such men as Tyr are hopelessly infected with the evil of the sun and are not fit to bear the sons of future Nor citizens. Bah! Those medics are soft from easy living, say I. The Gods have their ailments, and an easy, too well provided life, with too little danger, is one of them. For myself, I am determined to go my own way in this question of retrieving the sons of man from the Sun-evil.

I looked about for a second, deciding what to do next—not so Tyr. When he had locked the Angle in the cell safely, he had sprung back to our captive's ray-post and had swung the weapon around so as to cover the inside of the ship, rendering the whole craft visible to the screens within the post.

Before it had occurred to my reputedly superior mind to do so, Tyr had activated the sleeper ray—one ray which he knew was invisible—and had put half the ship's crew to sleep with it. Then, I took Tyr's place at the ray's controls, which was probably unwise, and swept the ship clean of conscious life.

I returned the view beam to its former position, angling slightly ahead to watch for other ships, when I saw a black shape cruising beside our own.

Scanning three hundred sixty degrees around the ship, I counted fifty of Sathanas' ships which had joined him since we had been captured.

"Oh-oh! This is a different problem entirely." I spoke to no one in particular. "This is going to require some thought."

I made one last swift search of the inside of what was now our ship, trying to find a trace of Arl. I failed. I had time for nothing more, for even though we had the flagship of Sathanas' fleet in our hands, that ship was surrounded by fifty of the enemy loyal to Sathanas, and more than willing to dispose of any Nortans—one Mutan Mion in particular. We had to get our ship out of there before we were discovered or be shot like roosting pigeons. At any moment one of the ships alongside of us would throw a view ray into the Satana for some purpose or other and our little game would be all over. I had no doubt that instant death would be our fate in the event of discovery.

Tyr again took the ray while I raced forward to the control bridge. It would have been too complicated for any of the Aesir to navigate this ship, and, besides, most of the weapons were too huge for anyone but the size of Arl or me. And where in the name of the Gods of Space was Arl?

Quickly I placed a mind control ray upon the ship's commander, one ugly fellow, Haltor by name. Standing him upon his feet by sheer strength of synthetic nerve-current command, I walked him toward the general televisor which was set to contact all of the ships of the fleet at once. I had him rasp out a few words as though in a great hurry at some sudden emergency.

"Commander Haltor to all ship commanders. Unforeseen emergency makes necessary a return to Earth for certain valuable material that was overlooked. The fleet will continue on its present course to destination. We will rejoin you as soon as we are able."

Not giving them time to question or to think about the orders, I swung the huge Satana in a short, tight arc that glued all of us to our seats under a half dozen gravities, and accelerated the ship on a return course. We were near a zone of weightlessness or the maneuver could not have been accomplished at the speed we were traveling. The High Commander Haltor I dropped unceremoniously to the deck where he resumed his interrupted slumber.

If I only had used that time of the return to Mu to everlastingly eliminate the 'great' Sathanas. But one's mind never functions correctly near Old Sol. One should figure out what to do, then do the opposite, when near this sun. I had decided to take Sathanas and his crew to Mu and leave them in the hands of the Aesir as a means of education for themselves. They could use the minds under telemach telaugs for a ready reference library of space travel and other needed information, and in a year or more be ready for a migration to a more beneficient energy field on some other planet. It was not a perfect solution to my problems, for Sathanas was not disposed of as the Nor Elders would have wished, but it did justice to the Aesir, and at the same time made it unnecessary for me to stay an illegal length of time upon the Earth.

But some ray from the fleet had caught a glimpse of the sleepers who should not have been sleeping, in tumbled positions everywhere about the ship. As I accelerated full back upon the return trail, out behind me I could see the fleet winging sharply around to turn upon me. Now I was the hunted. I prayed for the sight of a Nor patrol ship, but nothing showed in any direction. The ships behind me formed a 'V' of pursuit— being the quarry, I had the unpleasant feeling the formation was a spear point poised at my back. I was nearly helpless, for the massive guns of the great ship were not built to be fired by small men, or a few men, and I myself had to stay at the ship's controls. But I could leave her under robot control while I left for a short time to swing the big guns of the turrets for the smaller Aesir to fire. This I did and ran up into the master turret and swung a huge dis-ray in a vicious circle at the trailing ships. They did not want too close a taste of this. It was probable that the whole fleet was so built that this one ship could dominate it, for Sathanas did have sense enough to know that the type of men he used would be the type of men apt to find a reason to turn upon any domination. But they did not drop the pursuit. I might have shaken off one ship by a series of swift accelerations and change of course at each flash into invisibility of light speed, but to lose fifty pursuers was too much to expect. Too, it is dangerous to try complete acceleration thusly, for one may have miscalculated the weight in the haste of battle, and the figures on the sheet, suddenly resolved into actual force in the driver plates, would smear us against the metal walls—just so much human hash. In full speed flight, such maneuvers can be suicide without full checking by several sharp minds for error.

The ship began to heat under the combined fire of the rays from the whole circle of pursuit. I had to do something fast. The old hostage gag was in my mind, but would these pursuers care what happened to Sathanas, or would they seize the excuse to make me rid them of their master? Well, I would soon find out.

I sped into the sealed chamber which Sathanas used to bask in his special nutrient and stimulative pleasures. About him lay his women in sleep and upon a bed of spikes from which still coruscated the blue fire of synthetic pain, lay one of the women in torture. I had time to throw the switch on the pain juice, for no sleeper ray could have put that torture distended body to sleep. Now I understood Sathanas. He was an ordinary idiot like Ex-Elder Zeit, who must always be plaguing some poor devil to death. And no man can do much thinking if he is always busy torturing some unlucky mortal.

I drew the flame sword I had appropriated from one of the sleepers who was my size. Holding its point a little way from his breast, I gave his sleeping body a slight taste of its potent destructive power. He screamed into wakefulness. Such screams from a full grown man—a God almost. A bystander would have thought I hurt him. Maybe I did cause him pain at that—I hope so.

"Now, you overgrown hunk of diseased meat," I ordered him. "Will you call off that fleet or must I kill you?" I activated the telescreen beside the dais and upon it appeared the fleet, a great crescent of powerful shapes. "Step up and speak!"

Sathanas was suddenly reasonable. He stepped to the screen and showed himself. "It may be best for you to fall back away out of range, while the lord of Mandark under Van of Nor has time to discuss a little business with me. You can use the time to dispatch that little package of stuff on its way to the rendezvous. I can use it if it is safely there. I am a hostage and his terms must be understood."

The fire from the fleet ceased. It was none too soon, either. Probably they had supposed Sathanas was dead as well as the crew. Although the hull was not pierced, many of the sleepers had died from the rays upon us. They dropped away from us swiftly. Soon they were but hovering dots upon the far ray-view horizon, hundreds of miles astern. I kept the televisor upon the fleet. There was little discussion among them. They were just awaiting my next move. One ship moved off from the fleet and returned again upon the course we had just traveled along. Quickly I learned the reason for this action. Putting the question into the mind of one of the officers of the distant fleet, I was struck dumb by his answer, automatic and unconscious as I knew the thought was to him. I couldn't believe it. The mystery of our fruitless search for Arl aboard ship suddenly became clear to me. The answer in the man's mind was: "The ship is taking the great bodied queen of the giant Mutan Mion, beautiful Arl, to the place where women are made into love machines and automatons of the pleasure science. She will be a valuable stim operator after her will is removed and the will to pleasure only placed in her. Her beauty will be much sought after by the great ones. I wish I was getting the money someone will get for her from the dark ones of the evil palace of pleasure science."

Arl! It couldn't be another. And she was being taken from me. While I was still digesting the horrible facts, the ship disappeared.

Footnotes

22 NUTRIENTS: These nutrients are based on the hydrogen ion flow in the body. Most of the electric by which the greatest electrical machine known (human body) operates is borne about the body as a charge upon a flow of hydrogen ions. The ancients had developed a method of superimposing upon the hydrogen ion charges of certain energy flows not electric as we know it. These were borne into the body upon rays, where they become a part of the charge upon the hydrogen ion flow within the body's batteries, and are there borne to all the functioning parts of the flesh to be absorbed directly by the flesh. These rays—nutrient in nature—were formed directly from energy ash, the stuff of which all matter is formed. As well they had

methods of ionizing and rendering absorbable by the body such nutrients as we call vitamins. These volatile essences of nutrient foods they ionized and introduced into the blood stream as "nutrient rays"—driven through the air by electric pressure and sometimes by super-sonic force. These ions were charged in a complementary way that made them attractable by the ordinary body electric charge.—Author.

CHAPTER X.

A SATANIC HOSTAGE

I looked at Sathanas' face as he heard me read the man's thought over the distance telaug beam. He leered his sardonic and famous smile which he used only when he counted coup over some enemy. I juiced him a little with the flame sword and he sank half dead at my feet. I had lost all sympathy for the romance of evil as personified by Sathanas. He cost too much to have around. Arl was lost to me forever, unless I regained her soon, for a woman's soul cannot be replaced in her body once it is removed from her mind. I might get Arl back, but it did not look as though she would be anything but a smiling automaton to my wishes—a woman without volition or real thought. Well, I would regain her, anyway. Some Arl would be better than no Arl. I said as much to Sathanas: "So you prefer your woman in the condition in which you are putting my Arl. Yet, you do me the favor of doing the same thing to my Arl who was always too self-willed for my comfort. You have done me a favor, Sathanas, for which I will show my gratitude in due time. Meanwhile, stop that leering, I don't like it. A flame sword is a weapon that throws off a red flaming beam of destructive ions in any direction it is pointed," I explained to his agonized face, "and just now it is pointed at you, so don't try being so very clever. Even a God's patience can be exhausted by a fool's asinine facial expression." Sathanas altered his leering.

Meanwhile I had a problem on my hands. There was nothing I could do about Arl except try to heal her again once I got her back. The hovering fleet was just awaiting my next move. So was I. I had to keep Sathanas in my hands. I dosed him with sleeper beams to quiet the contortions of his face, then I turned toward the ship's controls keeping us headed for Mu. I didn't use any more speed. In his present state, Sathanas was no gift for the Aesir, and I had the fleet hot on my heels. I sat down to think.

At last it struck me! My ship, the Darkome, was the answer. It lay where I had left it, if the crew had followed my orders. I could not try to contact the Nor patrol by radio from the Satana, as the wave lengths of the apparatus were known and watched by the pursuing fleet. To try this would only invite attack by Sathanas' ships. Their allegiance to their master would not be so great that they would wait quietly by while I called the whole strength of vast Nor down upon them. I knew that it was only because I had not attempted this that they did not continue their attack in spite of my threat upon their master's life. But, if I could set a course near enough to the Darkome, if the crew of the waiting ship were on the alert and saw the whole string of enemy ships course overhead, and if none of the ships of Sathanas' saw the dark shape of the Darkome in the shadows of the rocks of the moon's surface, if all these things worked out correctly, then the Darkome would contact the Nor patrol over our secret wave lengths and the fleet behind us couldn't possibly have the slightest idea of any strategy.

If the Darkome lay where I had placed her, well under the shadow of a mighty meteor crater's wall, it was possible that the fleet could pass overhead without detecting her presence—unless the crew had placed a light for my guidance. That worried me—but I had given orders not to do so. The ordinary space radio is on a wave length known to everyone, but for secret communication the radio panel of Nor war ships contained several switches for different types of messages, and the radio, after such switches were thrown, operated on a wave length known to none but the construction men on the home planet. The receivers were also set up in the same manner so that secret messages could be heard only by commanders of ships of the intelligence branch according to which switch was set for the broadcast. Too, directional beam transmission cut down the chance of the message being intercepted by the Satanists. It might work. I stepped on the plate dis-flow button, my speed shot up to an uncomfortable acceleration. We shot past the moon, right over the Darkome's position. Whether she lay where I last left her or had gone in search of me, I could not tell. The place was all in the dark shadow of the mountains of the moon. I could not drop a beam to her without betraying her position. If she lay there, and if the fleet behind me failed to observe her, the chances were good that Nor ships would soon be coming toward our position at a good hundred light speeds. The men of the Darkome would hardly miss the sight and thunder of our drivers overhead. This was my only chance for escape from this Arch-fiend whose power over me still held, though he lay nearly dead at my feet.

Now, my problems were multiplied. First, I had to complete the capture and death of Sathanas. Second, I had to rescue my Arl from a secret stronghold of sin, the location of which I hadn't the faintest idea. Third, I had to turn over a brain to the Aesir for them to use to escape the sun-age death which I had sworn would not consume them. To stop me were the fifty great ships of war waiting impatiently overhead for me to conclude my conference with Sathanas and release him and his ship. It was ridiculous of them but they apparently expected me to strike a bargain with Sathanas and to take his word for a contract while I went about my business. Such is evil thought—ridiculous upon analysis. It was obvious to me that there was no way for me to release Sathanas from my hands except by death. I couldn't trust his word in the slightest; yet, to a logical man, there was no other thing that fleet was waiting for. Then they could come flaming in with all rays blasting. Some of them would have died. But certainly so would have the Satana and myself and her master gone up with her. What was I supposed to do with him—in their minds? I can never understand evil.

Why didn't they give the ship a flood of sleeper ray? Because we would have gone spinning down to Earth and not one of them could have stopped our fall, for the weight of the great ship was too much for their cargo magnetic grapple rays. The truth was that they were just waiting and so was I. Well, I had more to wait for than they, but they didn't know it. It is possible, too, that they thought me fool enough to trust the word of their master to release me and to restore Arl in return for his life.

Why didn't I kill him? I thought I might have to reenact the threat scene with the flame sword at his breast over the televisor to convince them I still meant business, and while that possibility existed, keeping him alive was a good investment.

I could not land the ship on Mu, for if a sleeper beam was used on the whole ship, Sathanas and I would have been taken alive.

I hung the ship on her driver beams' balance at fifty miles over the rocks and waited. But, I kept my hand on the controls in such a way that should a sleeper beam drop me unconscious, the ship would drop with me. We waited while I kept up a running fire of conversation with the now awakened Sathanas. Quickly I figured out these angles and awakened him as I saw my safety lay in pretending to dicker with him for some understanding. The fool believed me and was promising to set me off at Quanto, a base that was safe for him to approach, not being heavily defended, and leave me there after he had returned Arl to me. He assured me that the place where she had been sent was not far away. But, I knew as well as I know Arl's face, that he was lying. I did not have to look at the telaug needles to see the false needle vibrating in the red zone of der thought. No truth ever comes out of a man when he is in der, and all of Sathanas' thoughts were full of der—I knew that quite well. Yet, the man could live and other men could follow him. Why won't men study the lessons provided them to help them over the ever present opposition of dero which they are continually warned against? I can tell you—they are another kind of errant—a mentally blinded errant who cannot see because they will not look. Why don't they look? Because the der is in their will, too. How could Nor men have a der will when it is checked for continually? Because Sathanas, whose defection was hidden from the medicos by his doting family, had put the der will in them himself with cleverly contrived de-stim rays. After they had been fully infected with the deadly radioactivity, they had been ripe for his plans. How could Sathanas know so much about der as to use it on his own men to make them tractable to his will, and yet not understand the need for removing the radio-active material from his mind that caused his own err. Because Sathanas was mad, and a madman is not logical. 'Der' is a good thing to understand and I had studied it a long time.

Hanging there above old Mu, my four Aesir friends waiting with glum faces, I felt like a fly hung up in a spider web. But, somehow I knew that the wasp was coming for these spiders. Standing at the controls, I would doze for an instant, and the great Satana would start her long deadly plunge to the surface of Earth. The sudden drop would awaken me, or the Aesir would shake me awake and I would bring the ship back to its former position. Still faintly dotting the far ray-view horizon lay the fleet of the Satanists watching their master's ship. Sooner or later they would figure out that there was nothing to wait for, and would speed off, for there was no other choice left to them. They could do him no good now, for his fate was in my hands. As this became clear to their officers, one by one they deserted the vigil, flashing out of sight into immense speed to . . . to where? I wish I knew. Some of them would be smoked out in a hurry once I got my hands on the Darkome again.

At last I saw what I was waiting for—the Dread.Nors of the Nor Patrol suddenly swooping out of the invisibility of light speed into the visible ranges of movement as they braked their fight between the Moon and Earth where braking could be done without danger from weight's inertia. It can seem like magic—this speeding from weightless point of space to weightless point at the speed of many light velocities. One instant you are here, and the next your ship has arrived . . . if the automatic ultrafast relays have tripped your drive and brake rockets correctly. If they fail, you would not live to talk about it. It is delicate stuff to plot such courses—to handle shiploads of men whose lives hang on their hair-breadth of mental coordination necessary to set all the instruments aright before you take your course. To avoid disastrous inertia at start and stop is a feat, indeed.

Instantly, the patrol went into action. A moment before, the sky had been completely empty, then, suddenly, the Nor-ships appeared—guns blasting at the Satanists, like ships coming from the fourth dimension of ultra-speed into the three dimensions of visible speeds. One by one the ships of Satan's fleet dropped blazing into the seas of Earth. I grinned down at the semi-conscious Sathanas. "It seems that I win, O Lord of Foolishness and Evil, who turns on better men than himself who have done him no wrong. Soon your fleet will be no more. What do you think they will do with you?"

I gave his head a little ben-ray so that he would be able to answer me and able to realize and suffer from the realization of his position. His answer was a snarl of hatred. "You may have won this time, but there will come another day, Mutan Mion."

"If I know my Nor leaders, there will be no other day. However, you can win my support if you tell me where they have taken Arl. I will claim you as my captive and make sure that you live if you tell me where I can find my beloved."

Sathanas, as I had known he would, caved in immediately and told me the position of the pleasure science center where Arl had been taken. Although he had probably sworn a dozen mighty and terrible oaths not to reveal to Nor men any detail of the place, he did so at the first sign that it might be of value in saving his life. And like all evil men, he expected me to keep my word to one who would betray a trust without any provocation. Why? Because he knew my reputation as a man who keeps his word. Well, to keep that reputation, which at times has a great value, I would keep my word to the Arch-fiend. I would save him and turn him over to the Aesir as a walking map of the heavens where his evil life would at least find a use—a real use in making Gods and immortals out of worthy mortals.

As I wrote down the position of the place Sathanas described, I qualified my promise. to him. "However, I promise that you will never again lead men to death . . . you are through with power."

The remaining ships of the Satanists' fleet raised the signal of surrender and were herded in beside our own floating giant which had hoisted the white flag as the first blast of power from a Nor driver was seen on the detectors. In less time than it takes to tell, the Satana was swarming with clean cut men in the smart, glittering uniforms of the Nor Patrol—efficiency and law backed up by cool shiny dis guns, and ordered in clipped stern voices.

The Satanists never had a chance once their position we known. And well they knew it, too. I was never so glad to see anyone as that sharpfaced young officer who boarded us and cheerfully rubbed my position in to me. I showed him the mighty Sathanas coiled up in an agonized heap of epilepto-ray-charge, for I had no desire of a reputation for softness among the patrol man, and had dosed him with epilepto-ray as they drew alongside. His smile of triumph was very warm and pleasant. He fully understood the predicament he had rescued me from and I knew that he never intended to forget this episode. "'How Mion got hold of the devil and couldn't let go . . . '" was the story I would hear many times before I moved on to the heavy planets.

"Opportune, our arrival, wasn't it, sir? You are the Earthman, Mutan Mion of Nor, now of Van of Nor? Yes, I know much of you, but I have never had the pleasure of meeting you."

I shook his hand, not minding the implied sarcasm. "Yes, you saved me from a nasty situation. I was captured by the big fellow as I returned from a trip to Earth. We managed to take the ship from his crew just as this fleet showed up to the rendezvous here. We were safe because we still held Sathanas alive, but how to let go—how to get away from that bunch of armored battlewagons, I couldn't figure."

"Well, I guess it's all over now. We have only to take his nibs back to Nor and turn him and his remaining followers in." The young officer's face was greatly relieved that there was no more trouble in this affair for him. But I dashed his hopes.

"That's not entirely true, my friend. A few hours ago he sent my Lady Arl to a place that is called the "Pleasure Science Center." She is to be the victim of a mind degrading operation, and afterward is to be sold as a slave to some commercial pleasure palace of the illegal type. Much of Sathanas' business was of this pandering kind and we are apt to find many a maid of Nor there who has been or will be changed into the sort of animal Sathanas prefers around him. We have no choice but to attack the place, however far or however strong it may be, according to the oath we swear when we take service under the Nor flag. Remember the words: 'To uphold the honor of Nortan womanhood at the expense even of our life or reason—to risk all dangers for the sake of extending the rule of reason through all space . . . '"

"I did not know, Lord Mion. The businesses of Sathanas are much larger than Sathanas, that I do know. But of the Lady Arl or of any other Nor maidens who are in their hands, I did not know. Where is this place they have sent her? We must prepare an attack, of course, but that is something we must not rush headlong into. We know little about the strength of these illegal cults. They have only been uncovered among the Nor since the exposure of Sathanas."

"There is no time for the usual procedure of preparation for war. They will start work on Arl at once after she arrives. I don't intend to wait for that to happen. I have the position of the place. To get this, I bargained with Sathanas, promising him his life for the information. If he has lied, he dies. He is going to accompany me so that I may read his mind en route and learn all he knows of the thing. Whether or not you and the ships under your command accompany me is up to you or your superior officer at the base. The Darkome is under my command and the Darkome leaves at once to rescue Arl from the place called the Center of the Science of Pleasure. Its true name is more correctly the Place of Evil Lust, or it should be. Sathanas' ship and his own ugly self are both mine by right of capture, according to the Code of Nor. So, I have two ships to fling at this focus of evil."

"Where is the place?" asked the young commander—young to me, meaning he was but a century or two my junior. He was my senior in the patrol, but I was not under his command. In the Nor Military Organization, a man is responsible only to those officers who are designated over him, that is, I could be overruled by him only after he reported to my superiors.

"It lies on the rim of the light of Fomalhaut, twenty some light years from this spot. Fomalhaut, itself, can be reached in four days accelerating from the zone of weightlessness between Saturn and Jupiter—in this system, Saturn and Jupiter are the sixth and fifth planets from the sun, respectively. At steady acceleration, we should reach fourteen hundred light speeds in a few hours. It is unwise to accelerate to a greater rate for such a short trip, so it will take us four days."

"Four days seems like a lot of time for even a short trip like this one," countered the young commander.

"Under normal circumstances that would be true, but 1 want to decelerate out of the ultra speeds near the sub-planet Pandral—but not too near. That's what will take the time."

"Pandral, Lord Mion? I can't recall ever having heard of it before."

"Neither had I until I read Sathanas' mind—but that is where these fiends have taken the Lady Arl—and that's where I am determined to go—alone, if need be."

"You will not have to go alone, Lord Mion—but, first, let us take another look at Sathanas' brain. If the place looks vulnerable, we will chance it. If not, we will report the place—and then scout it for the arrival of a real battle force."

I shook the man's hand. He was not over-cautious or too subservient to ritual—the only mark of evil that one can find in the clean race of the Nor. He was a man. We set the course at once and blasted off into the ultra speed that is used on such journeys. Some eighty light speeds we attained at one jolt from the center of no-weight between Moon and Earth. I set the pursuit needle to seek out the trail of the ship that had borne Arl away to her 'life of pleasure' as these fiends ironically called condemning a human to a mindless life of slavery to evil desire. With another set of blasts from the ro-pilot as we passed between Saturn and Jupiter, we attained fourteen hundred light speeds—all that we required.

Then we put the telaug on Sathanas' mind and sat down to the job of examining every picture it contained that in any way related to our objective and the force that defended its evil existence. There was a great deal to know—to learn, we found. For many centuries this place—its true name was Pandral—had been in the business of manufacturing and peddling slaves for the Hell-holes of the rims of the Nor Empire. Like every great empire, Nor's sway extended only so far, and where her authority stopped, there lived her parasites, those who pandered to the thoughtless sybarites of the Empire who sought outside Nor what could not be obtained where her law prevailed. The very absoluteness and thoroughness of Nor police work gave them their opportunity, for those thirsts of evil origin could not be quenched in Nor, but those who thirst will drink some way, and so Normen themselves supported their worst enemies—just as they do in less intelligent worlds.

CHAPTER XI.

PLOT AGAINST PANDRAL

Pandral was a planetoid about two thousand miles in diameter. To the eye, it was a lifeless ball, but so are all Nor planets and planetoids. There is not much use in their concealment, and the modern Nor are dropping the custom, but the ancient precaution of concealing all surface work to cut down the value of enemy observation from the exterior still exists, though there are few enemies for Nor to worry over any more. Within, Pandral was an exquisitely designed pleasure palace—all two thousand miles of it—honeycombed with the chambers that the life science of Nor knows so well how to build—honeycombed with the caverns of. our Ancient Race as is Mother Mu. Within these vast chambers where all imaginable conditions of life are reproduced, life was studied, not for what value could be made of it, but for what could be made from it for profit—what attractions could be created which the nature of man would be unable to resist. This creation of bait for the sucker was the prime purpose of Pandral's existence. They did not create pleasure for itself; they created lures on which the rich fish would inevitably bite. Once hooked, the fish was exposed to their blackmail which was the source of their profit. He had no way of retaliating for fear of exposure to the Nor police system, and so Pandral extracted a great part of the income from the pockets of the weaker great of Nor. This process of milking Nor had gone on so long that it was practically taken for granted as not really evil but a natural result of the existence of fools with money in their pockets—and no prosperous nation can avoid creating bulging pockets—even those of fools. But, the true evil of Pandral was very carefully hidden beneath a vast network of subtle propaganda and more sinister fear of their strength which kept those mouths closed which might have remedied the evil. This was the cover which hid the business of creating those creatures which Sathanas had so great a taste for—those without minds except in the pursuit of pleasure. Well, be that as it may, we knew what Pandral was, but did nothing about it for the reason that they were very careful about whom they hurt and had so far managed to avoid antagonizing anyone strong enough to trim their spreading power. It was high time, I realized, that more was known of these dives which grew so prolifically about the far spread boundaries of the Nor Empire. Again I was struck by a thing I can never understand—how can great minds make such fearful mistakes? Here was Nor, with the greatest minds of space at her helf, surrounded by festering evil which she apparently did not even know existed. But, then, did I know those minds I so firmly believed in? No. I only believed in them because I knew a few such minds as the Princess Vanue's. Again I was struck with my own ignorance in not realizing that even Nor had her ailments, and that this ailment must be chalked up to failure in her upper strata.

Pandral was well defended, in Sathanas' mind, both by ships and fixed batteries of rays far too powerful for any strength we had on our handful of ships—not quite two hundred powerful battlewagons, true, but no match for the strength we saw built into the stones of Pandral. We could not take the place by storm; we must take it by a strategem.

I had a ready means of entry in the person of Sathanas who was known there. If I could retain control over him when I got within their ray—that was the problem. It would not be pleasant to be exposed by Sathanas within the power of Pandral's forces, for their fear of Nor would make our demise swift.

Using Sathanas' mind for continual reference, I disguised myself as a certain friend of his, Profir, by name, who had been killed in the action.

He was about my size and fair, but we worked on the disguise carefully to make it correspond with Sathanas' mental images. Then, we dressed Sathanas' locks with care, crowning our handiwork with a golden circlet, studded with gems, within which was a powerful little mental radio which kept the commands from my own telaug imposed upon his thought in such strength that there was no danger of his using his own will. My telaug and control device were concealed in a great metal studded belt I wore, from which hung a flame sword and a powerful dissociator pistol ray. More weapons would have disclosed our purpose. I counted on their familiarity with Sathanas. Making up a party of twenty, which was about the number usually in Sathanas' parties on his visits here, we readied the Satana for a close look from examining ray. The crew was dressed in the uniforms of the captive crew, and carefully prepared mentally by hypnosis for their part as men whose allegiance was Sathanas'. However, a certain device was readied for general energy flows which would be released by me if at any time I needed their full minds for combat. When everything was ready, the Satana shot off to enter the watching ray beams of the pirate stronghold. If all went well, it would be the last time a ship would enter that place of mutilation. No more would minds of immortals be changed into the tools of fools. If I could hit that hole at all, I would not cease until it was a cinder floating in space, empty of life.

The place we entered had the reputation among those who frequented the illegal dens as the most glamorous and the most dangerous of them all. We entered, the huge form of Sathanas in the lead and myself towering a little higher just behind him. The twenty stout fellows took up positions behind us where any attack could be shot at without interfering with each other. Thus protected at the back, we advanced down the tremendous hall. I knew that the people who ruled this place would not be glad to see Sathanas, knowing of his flight from the Nor Patrol. It was obvious that they welcomed anyone who was outside the law as a matter of general practice—and so, they could hardly refuse the great Sathanas one of the biggest gears in this machinery of space-wide vice.

An obsequious female prostrated herself before us. "My Lords, may I bid you welcome?"

With a sneer, and in his typically ungracious manner, Sathanas spoke:

"We will speak with 'the Boss', My Lord Harald."

It didn't sound like he held much respect or affection for this Harald—the way his voice dripped when he spoke his name. I, meanwhile, held my fingers tightly crossed under my cape, hoping that we were going through the usual Sathanas routine. Otherwise our little game would soon be terminated—perhaps fatally.

I sensed that something was going wrong and I'd better find out what it was and soon. I focused my telaug on the poor wretch who now was standing, puzzled before us. In her mind was bewilderment that the great Lord Sathanas hadn't gone at once to the chambers always held in readiness for the master of the Satana.

I made Sathanas speak: "Take me and my men to our rooms."

Again that wonder that Sathanas wasn't following his usual practice, but she obeyed.

"Will my Lords follow me," she offered as she led the way out of the hall that we were in.

"Damn!" I thought, "how had I missed that entrance in Sathanas' mind?" I thought that I had covered everything when I read his thoughts about this place. I didn't know—or see—that he always met the big shot in the same place, in the same rooms.

True, I did know where the rooms were—but I wanted the girl to lead the way. She had wondered about things that, if somebody here in this palace had read in her mind, would have roused suspicion. We were in dangerous enough territory without having anything that we could cover give us away. This first step of ours had been a slip. I prayed to the gods of space for no more mistakes—another one might prove fatal.

One thing I knew. If it were usual for Sathanas to meet the Boss of this glorified den in some of the rooms in the immediate vicinity, then

I could keep the girl who brought us here with us without arousing any suspicion—keep her here where we could watch that she didn't repeat those thoughts of wonder that could have ruined our little plan.

So, as she showed us into a large chamber off the great hall, I grasped her arm.

"Little Dark Flower, stay with us. We have been far and your smile is pleasant. Will you dance for us?"

The poor creature looked up into my eyes with her's wet with gratitude that someone had noticed her among all the beautiful women from a score of strange planets. She was a pretty thing, about half my own height, alive with the lush dark beauty of the women from Bohan. Her natural charms had been enhanced and stimulated with the life influence that had been grown in her making her an instrument for men's pleasure.

She couldn't speak for the rare pleasure of being noticed. but I read her thoughts. Again wonder.

'A kind face among Sathanas' friends? Now, perhaps, I shall get a little stim. Everyone around here is so tight with me. They begrudge even the breath I draw.'

She glanced at me, and at my reassuring nod she pressed a wall stud that flooded the room with a strong vibrant ray of intense pleasure. Her face relaxed under it like one denied something a long time and then receiving it in abundance . . . something that was like the breath of life itself to her. I realized that stim replaced natural love with these maltreated creatures, that she loved those who gave her stim and had no emotions otherwise. Swiftly she shed her uniform, and donned a few slight spangles from a closet of female trappings in the wall. Then, adjusting a spot of stim ray, she placed it in my hand, telling me to keep it on her. I turned it up to full power, and her body writhed slowly, hands outstretched, as she warmed herself beautifully at the spot ray in my hands, begged and begged with her motions for a little indulgence, a little kindness. She was a master of the art of expressing her thoughts with her motions, and knowing her thoughts, I interpreted her motions correctly. Well, if I had my way, freedom or death would be her lot before long.

The rest of the party sprawled about the chamber on the rich divans, and bawled at the attendants for drinks and women, just as we had seen Sathanas' followers do in Sathanas' mental images. Soon they were well supplied with diversion. Before each of them writhed a dancer and on each side of them nestled a beauty amorously inclined. Music was supplied by a half dozen Amero youths, a race whose talent for music is superior to that of most races, and whose talent in other directions is singularly lacking. They are much used in their present capacityunintrusive musical accompaniment.

The party was really moving along at a deceptive pace when the gentleman we had come across vast stellar space to see appeared.

A well concealed door at the rear of the chamber that we were in, opened, and, like a huge lumbering mammoth from the swamps of Mu, the Chief himself ambled through. He was dressed as we formerly decked out the mammoths of Mu for the annual games in which the Titans delighted.

This portly creature was of some unguessable racial origin—horned like a Titan, but as fat and as ungainly corpulent as a hippopotamus. He was as tall as I am, but I'll wager that he was thrice my weight. The fingers of the fat, pudgy hands swelled around many gaudy rings that his vain nature fancied. Reflecting the falsity and affectation of the many rings were his little gimlet eyes, sparkling with a sickly, unholy gleam through the generous folds of his too pig-like face. Pig eyes with the hidden, treacherous cunning of a fox somehow apparent within them. It had been many a year since I last slaughtered pigs on one of my estates on Mandark—but one look at this—this overstuffed imitation of a man, and my fingers itched to see a blade in my hand spread the fat folds of flesh on that accursed neck and send him to whatever lies beyond . . .

His name I knew from reading the mind of Sathanas. It was, unappropriately enough, Harald. He had no official tie with any government, though there were probably many that would have given a lot to get him if they knew that it was he that was the master mind behind this space-wide slave ring. Here, on his little unsavory ball of matter that polluted the reaches of space, he was known as the "Ruler of Pandral, Sir Harald".

Out of the mouth of Sathanas came the words that I willed him to say, though I nearly choked on the thought:

"Greetings, Sir Harald," spoke the voice of Sathanas as he stood up and approached the gross body of Harald, now seating himself in the best pile of cushions as gracefully as a space freighter settling to a port with half its lifters gone.

"Ugh . . . ugh . . ." the fat frog croaked.

"Sir Harald," Sathanas continued, "I have several matters that I wish to talk over with your Grace."

"His Grace" paused in his stuffing his fat mouth with some delicacy or another, to deign to raise an eyebrow and question, "Oh . . . yes?"

"The price of the little morsel that I sent you . . . the Lady Arl." I made Sathanas rub his hands as he would have, no doubt, if he were acting on his own volition.

"And the other matters?"

I thought to myself at this, 'The old buzzard can talk then, if it interests him.'

"The other matter," said Sathanas, answering Harald's question, "is our future plans, now that I am no longer numbered among the pillars of virtue of Nortan society."

As the Ruler of Pandral rearranged the folds of his crimson silken garments around him before continuing the talk with me, or as he thought, with Sathanas, Sathanas had to move as my mind ordered. There was this bloated thing before us, a thing that should not be insultingly alive and moving where we could see him.

The other parts of the plot were moving as we had planned. While Sathanas and Harald were talking, the rest of the men were disporting themselves with Harald's slaves. Some of them were feigning drunkenness and others merely were acting half drunk—making a clumsy attempt to dance and cavort with the girls they had chosen.

Two of the latter, among the biggest in our crew, managed to dance with their prizes behind the spot where sat Sathanas, Harald, and myself, presumably Sathanas' second in command.

So smoothly and quickly that the others in the room weren't aware of what was happening, our two suddenly stopped dancing and in a trice had the obese Harald, as he began to answer me in their iron embrace, and a circlet exactly like the one encircling Sathanas' head was clapped upon his head. Instantly he relaxed, his will now was overpowered by a flood of synthetic nerve impulse from a teleradio within the belt of my lieutenant. Sir Harald was now a servant of a brain not his own. No impulse his brain could generate would be powerful enough to overrule the steady flow of power from an instrument ruled by another mind.

"Can you read him?" I asked Tyron, my lieutenant. "Easily," he answered.

"Ask him what would be the thing he would do ordinarily when he left this apartment, if nothing had occurred."

"He would have gone directly to his own apartments to think over his talk with Sathanas and decide what was best to do. Then he would return to this chamber to tell Sathanas what he had decided."

"Did he ever take Sathanas to these apartments?"

"Never," answered Tyron. This had happened so quickly that only two of the attendant sirens had noticed the brief contact which had resulted in Harald's loss of control. Those were suddenly overcome by a sudden inexplicable drunkenness emanating from a tiny gun in my sleeve. I examined the rest of the poor fair heads to see if they realized what had occurred, but the only two who had seen were those who were dancing with our two champions who had slipped the circlet on Harald's head.

The situation, Tyron went on to explain, necessitated that we go to Harald's apartments for they were filled with apparatus which controlled the whole stronghold. I thought it best to dismiss the rest of the heterae before they overheard the strong mental conversation we were carrying on without their knowing it.

"We'll have to risk it. Whether or not it is the customary thing to do, we're going to his apartments."

Sending Sathanas and Harald ahead, we strolled out of the chambers. Working the two controls, the obese Harold and Sathanas were engaged in animated conversation. Tyron and I came next. Behind us, the rest of the party casually strolled fanwise as before. After all, Harald had placed himself in our hands. It should not look unusual except to those whom we should meet within the ruler's private nest.

Nothing happened. Step after step, each seeming an age, and still nothing happened. We neared the ornate arch leading to Harald's private sanctum; nothing barred our way, no ray swept over us in revealing inquiry. Would one of their rays reveal the control I held over Harold and Sathanas or would it pass over, seeing nothing? The next few minutes would tell. It could be seen by alert men trained in the type of work to which we were accustomed, but did the outlaws have men trained as we were, or were they men who had picked up their training hit or miss? But, these were not the thoughts to think and I brushed them aside and filled my mind with visions of the choice beauties Harald was to show us for our entertainment during our stay here—of all the varied stim experiences which were to fill my days here—of all the delectable pleasures I vas going to sample. With anything but the truth I filled my mind's images.

Then we were in the luxurious lounges of the rich pirate's suite of rooms. The armed guards looked us over curiously. I made Sathanas talk: "I must see these new mechanisms for the conversion of character you have built. I must see their results in the living person, for I intend to buy a great many of them. I am building anew in a secret place."

My lieutenant made Harald answer: "Yes, you shall see many new things we have devised for the entertainment of the customers or victims, whichever they happen to be. We have created several new character types—several different fixed-idea mentalities which are extremely appealing to the desirous male."

Then it happened. The women there who were Harald's things noticed the circlet. Stupidly they called attention to it, asking among themselves, "What is that new head ornament Harald is wearing? I have never seen it before."

One of the guards heard the women's chatter and glanced at Harald's head. Noting that Sathanas wore the same kind of head circlet, the truth flashed into his mind as he looked at the rest of us and saw the space bronzed iron of the patrol warriors, the sharp, undissipated eyes, the clean, healthy flesh, not one soft, self-indulgent character among them. The incongruity of our health and intent gave us away to the man. He saw it all too plainly.

I shot him as he raised his voice to shout a warning. In an instant the rooms filled with a criss-cross of dissociator beams and the long flames of power swords reached at us from the rooms beyond. At the first bolt, we flung ourselves to the floor. The fire lasted but a minute, and the rooms were clear. Several of my men lay dead. As far as I could tell, the guards who had been there were also dead. I raced toward the inner rooms where the banks of control mech lay. I knew the whole stronghold could be ruled from these banks of instruments. I had carefully examined Harald's brain for the methods behind the mech that lay here. I reached the great permalloy door as it was almost swung to, and crashed my shoulder into it. Someone screamed beyond and the door opened. A man of small stature lay sprawled inert across the room where my charge had flung him. There were a half dozen in the room—females—aging creatures, too. Why age? I did not stop to ask, perhaps they were dupes of Harald's who had gained their allegiance with some promise of treatment.

They sat at the great multi-vision screens watching the life of the place for any untoward activity. How they missed our own was easy to explain. One man can't see everything, and we had not given them time to see much. I herded them into a corner and swiftly disarmed them.

Now for the last bit of trickery. If it failed, I probably would die here before the place could be taken by the waiting battle fleet. I called Harald and his controller into the room full of mech. Standing him before the multi-screens, Tyron made him give the message we had composed.

"Men, we are going to be inspected by the Nor patrol. Do not be alarmed. Everything is arranged between us and they will merely perform a routine and perfunctory inspection. Be on your guard that nothing happens while the patrol are about. We have nothing to hide from them. Be sure that nothing goes on while they are here that should be hidden from them. I give you five minutes to make ready for their arrival. Do not fire on the ships. Everything has been arranged between us."

On the screen, a sudden confused scramble marked the attempt to hide in five minutes, the tell-tale traces of illegal activities. I knew that they had been inspected before and would not think another inspection amiss, in spite of the short notice. It would have been unnatural for Harald to fight Nor men, for he could not hope to win in a long struggle. Obviously, he was submitting to a search. They had noted Sathanas' arrival and may have thought Harald had decided to give the Great Sathanas up rather than defend him from pursuit. Whatever they thought, the fleet blazed up to a stop before the landing cradles and settled to a landing.

Into the great locks trundled the patrol ships, one after the other. I knew that this was unusual in an inspection, as the ships hung outside, and a few officers did the inspecting, but I trusted the bustle of the five minute preparation to conceal the movement of the ships from general notice. The alarmed faces of several of Harald's men announced this unusual feature to Harald's visage on the screens, but Tyron made Harald gesture reassuringly and nothing further happened.

The men dispersed through the great fortress as they had been ordered. After an interval of waiting for all the batteries to be invested, I showed my face on the screen beside Harald's to see if all the batteries had been entered by Normen. They stood in readiness, disblasters in their hands, occupying each great battery of space guns that ordinarily would have made every attempt at assault useless. A wave of my hand and they arrested every officer of Harald's guard, and disarmed the rest, a Nor man placing himself at every gun. The place was in our hands with not a shot fired since Harald had announced our entry on the screens. Such is subterfuge—a sweet weapon when it works, a deadly one to the user when it fails. In order to use it we had to place a chunk of our fleet under their guns in complete helplessness. But everything had gone without mishap.

Now to find the Lady Arl before anything more happened to her. Leaving Tyron to run things, I took a dozen men and raced through the endless caverns of Harald's pleasure palace looking for the growth caverns where his creatures were manufactured out of normal flesh and blood.

CHAPTER XII.

HARALD'S HOSTAGES

Servants of evil men can be fiends. These were. In the growth caverns, many things that no man should see were going on. Little girls were being trained by ro-mech to be faultless dancers—automatons of rhythm. The process was designed to develop those muscles and thoughts needed by a dancer to the exclusion of other growth within her body. To attain this, she was wired to a thought record taken from some famous dancer's brain, and day after day, her little body mechanically repeated the motions and her brain mechanically repeated the thoughts of the dancer until the whole dance became automatism. A thing was produced which would never be human and a thing hard to describe to those who have not seen it.

These creatures were slaves. They had nothing whatever to say about their fate in any way. Much of the treatment was very beneficial; the slavers adopted the best medical science of the immortal races to gain their own ends. It was the unbalance of the character aimed at by such men as Harald and Sathanas that was evil.

There were hundreds of liquid nutrient tanks in which females of all sizes and races were suspended. Upon their brains telerays played, impressing repeatedly hypnotic commands as well as the whole gamut of erotic thoughts culled from millions of years of the development of the science of pleasure in just such gilded palaces of slavery. All this was extremely pleasant to the recipient, so much so as to crowd all other tendencies from their minds. They were given such treatment from the earliest childhood, if they fell into the hands of the slavers at that age. They received no other education. Thus, the art of pleasure was burned into their brains until they knew no other objective.

Through every pleasure nerve of the body ran nutrient and growth stimulating flows introduced directly into the nerves by tiny needles. The whole body immersed in the nutrient liquid, evolved a covering flesh more alive, more soft, more reactive to sensation than is the case in the normally developed human being.

Such women had many men passionately enslaved to them, giving them every penny of their income. All this went directly into the pockets of such as Harald. Naturally he never released any of these profitable slaves from his bondage.

Thus all the growth and life science of the vast races of immortals was here perverted in this evil world of Pandral to the ends of the master—power and gold. No one but Harald had a will in any matter on all Pandral but for the profit of the master.

The growth rays, if concentrated on those nerves which cause pleasure sensations, can give a person infinitely greater capacity for pleasure than in the normal person. But, when this is done, the ability to resist such pleasure does not grow normally and the creature becomes a servant to the will to pleasure. And, since the greatest pleasure comes from synthetic nerve impulse generators, they become a servant of the machine. While this could be a means of enhancing the joy of life in the proper hands, such men as Harald were certainly not the proper hands.

At last I found and released my beloved. I cannot tell you what had been done to her, but I have hopes of repairing the damage. She would have become a delectable morsel for some mad master, for what had been designed for her was not a choice future.

We herded the heterae, the drunken customers, the whole crew of unnatural servants aboard the captive vessels and dispatched them toward the courts of the Nor Empire. I will be there when their cases come up, and I will have plenty to say. Some of those child victims of his will yet grace Mandark after Vanue's laboratories are through with their reconstruction. Vanue's reward system will shake evil thought out of their beautiful young heads.

I said to Harald: "You think you can pervert the life stream of the race to your own selfish ends. Love is sacred to the Gods. Your manufacture of will-less sirens will not be appreciated by the courts such men hold in Nor for just your kind. It's only by accident that a youngster of my diminutive stature—a mere fifty feet of man—came upon your place in my pursuit of Sathanas. Had one of our leaders chanced upon information leading to this hole, your lot would have been different. Already you would have been dealt with. It pays to be virtuous so far as you can imagine virtue, for when one steps off the path, one faces these beings whom no power of our imagination could vision . . . no force we could conjure up would ever overcome, for their life is ages old and has been gaining in strength for all those years. Those who take a whole planet to build one home upon will not allow their laws to be set aside by any pipsqueak who conceives a new way to make money and fails to remember that the race is sacred to the Gods. You have forgotten that though the Gods must of necessity dwell afar, yet they do not forget their source. Some of the very creatures you have mutilated were kin of such mighty men, and if I had not caught up with you they would have, and your fate would have been far different from the trial and imprisonment I plan for you."

Harald made no answer, but only glared at me in furious frustration.

"The great ones always search for the young of the race for better brains to carry out their mighty plans, and they are not pleased with the pollution of the blood that bears their agents. They guard the tree of life, for they have a mighty use for its fruit. Even assuming they were evil, and it is sometimes true that they guard the tree for nothing better than to pick the beautiful fruit—the young females as they mature—still they are not pleased with the malformation—-the defiling of the tree that bears their much desired beauties to grace the harems of Gods. Even assuming the Gods themselves had no higher purpose than yourself, would you believe that they would allow you to pollute a tree that produced the agents of their immortal pleasures? Has it not seemed strangely easy for me to overcome your greater strength? We are probably flooded with the observation and control rays of mightier ones that we can imagine exist. How else could a man take a fortress like this with two simple mental radios and a couple of dis-guns? If you are ever free again, don't forget the Gods. One way to remain alive is to envision the will of the Gods and carry it out as if they were observing you, for sooner or later they will observe you. Go now, to central Nor and to trial for every ill deed you have worked against the life of Normen."

Pandral in the future will be a base for the Nor patrol. It is well suited to the purpose.

Once more I took Sathanas aboard the Satana. I instructed the four Aesir in the mind reading apparatus until I felt sure that nothing Sathanas knew would be lost to them. Then setting them on their course for Earth, I abandoned them to their pursuit of knowledge they would get from Sathanas. The arch-fiend was immobilized by a nerve operation I performed. There is little danger that he will get out of hand on Earth before the Aesir have used him for the purpose to which I dedicated the rest of his misused life. He will serve as a map and a guide to the operations of the ships the Aesir will need for a migration to the dark spaces beyond the deadly light of any sun. And when the Aesir soar at last into the starless dark, Sathanas will lie in chains in one of the deepest pits of the forgotten cities beneath the Earth's crust. May he lie there forever.

... and Satan did lie there forever, as Dante tells us, but he succeeded in being a curse to man in spite of his chains.

THE END

MR. SHAVER'S LEMURIAN ALPHABET

A—Animal (used AN for short)
B—Be (to exist—often command)
C—See
D—(also used DE) Disintegrant energy; Detrimental (most important symbol in language)
E—Energy (an all concept, including motion)
F—Fecund (use FE as in female—fecund man)
G—Generate (used GEN)
H—Human (some doubt on this one)
I—Self; Ego (same as our I)
J—(see G) (same as generate)
K—Kinetic (force of motion)
L—Life
M—Man
N—Child; Spore; Seed (as ninny)
O—Orifice (a source concept)
P—Power
Q—Quest (as question)
R—(used as AR) Horror (symbol of dangerous quantity of dis force in the object)
S—(SIS) (an important symbol of the sun)
T—(used as TE) (the most important symbol; origin of the cross symbol) Integration; Force of growth (the intake of T is cause of gravity; the force is T; tic meant science of growth; remains as credit word)
U—You

V—Vital (used as VI) (the stuff Messmer calls animal magnetism; sex appeal)
W—Will
X—Conflict (crossed force lines)
Y—Why
Z—Zero (a quantity of energy of T neutralized by an equal quantity of D)

Some "English" Lemurian Words

ABSENT—Animal be sent (one was sent, therefore is not here)
ADDER—A der (the animal is a der. or deadly)
ARREST—Animal stops to rest (the ar syllable means is dangerously stopped)
BEGET—To cause to exist (command to generate the energy of inteorance)
BAD—Be a de (to be a destructive force)
BARD—Bar de (one who allays depressing de force, who over-joys us, decreases depression)
BIG—Be I generate (in the act of generation, as pregnant)
BILK—Be ill kinetic (to run away from ill, to dodge—K for movement)
DARK—Detrimental horrible movement (harrowing things we are apt to see "in the dark")
DECEASE—Stopped by de (disintegrated to the noint of ceasing to be—death)
DEVIATE—De vital ate (de has eaten the vital force. implicatiot. being the thing goes astray he-cause of destructive force)
DEVIL—De vile (to be vile with de; completely destructive)
DROP—De ro power (disintegrance governs power, thus it becomes less, falls)
LADY—Lay de (allay depression; complimentary term)

MAD—Man a de (one who may de, be apt to destroy)
MEAN—Me animal (animal conscious only of self)
MORBID—More be I de (I don't want to be any more, I want to die)
NEE—Child energy (charm)
NEUTRAL—Ne you to ral (attracted by the charm of both parties)
OBSCENE—Orifice see charm (orifice meant source of life, thus the meaning is evident)
PACT—Power act (an empowered act)
PEAL—Power all (power and all combine to give a loud sound)
PRISON—Price on (to hold for ransom)
QUIT—Quest you I to (get someone else to do good)
VAN—Vital animal (the leader)
ZEAL—Zero all (foolish ardor to zeal)

p 146 - Charles Fort
Journal of American Folk Lore
The Book of the Damned
Wild Talents p 148
p 127 Present Day Humans

BIBLIOBAZAAR

The essential book market!

Did you know that you can get any of our titles in large print?

Did you know that we have an ever-growing collection of books in many languages?

Order online:
www.bibliobazaar.com

Find all of your favorite classic books!

Stay up to date with the latest government reports!

At BiblioBazaar, we aim to make knowledge more accessible by making thousands of titles available to you- *quickly and affordably*.

Contact us:
BiblioBazaar
PO Box 21206
Charleston, SC 29413